DS 481 .G3 5

W9-APO-337

The Mahatma and the World

Books by

KRISHNALAL SHRIDHARANI

In English

WAR WITHOUT VIOLENCE
MY INDIA, MY AMERICA
WARNING TO THE WEST
THE MAHATMA AND THE WORLD

In Gujarati

THE BANYAN TREE *(Vadalo)*
A Nature Fantasy

I SHALL KILL THE HUMAN IN YOU!
(Insan Mita Dunga)
A Novel of Life in Jail

SPRING FLOWERS *(Pila Palash)*
Three Plays for Children

THE SUTTEE *(Padmini)*
A Historical Play

THE EGGS OF PEACOCK *(Morna Inda)*
A Social Play

THESE EARTHEN LAMPS *(Kodiya)*
A Collection of Poems

THE MAHATMA
AND THE WORLD

BY KRISHNALAL SHRIDHARANI

DUELL, SLOAN AND PEARCE · NEW YORK

LIBRARY
SOUTHERN SEMINARY

921
G 15 sh

Sept 44

Copyright, 1946, by
Krishnalal Shridharani

All rights reserved, including
the right to reproduce this book
or portions thereof in any form

SECOND PRINTING

PRINTED IN THE UNITED STATES OF AMERICA
AMERICAN BOOK-STRATFORD PRESS, INC., NEW YORK

6692

*To my American friends,
in every walk of life,
of each State in the Union,
a parting salute*

Inspiration for a Portrait

The Lord Supreme and Parvati I praise,
The parents of all worlds, close-joined in one
As word with sense, and pray for gift of speech
With mighty meaning fraught. How else could I,
Weak-witted, dare to hymn the kingly race
Descended from the Sun—daring not less
Than one who ventures on a raft to cross
Some pathless sea?

THUS prayed Kalidasa, the classical Sanskrit poet, before penning his life of Rama the Avatara. I see him sitting under a banyan tree as he embarked upon the project, attuned to the speaking silence of a forest looking up at the endless expanse of the deep blue Indian sky, and silently attended by his pet deer.

In the hearts of most Hindus Mahatma Gandhi, my subject, is no less in the line of prophetic tradition than Rama was. And though Kalidasa had a raft, I have only a straw with which to keep afloat on the wide and bottomless sea. My inspiration comes from modern men instead of the ancient gods and amidst the turmoil-filled canyons of steel and cement and glass which squeeze the New York sky into narrow ribbons.

[vii]

LIBRARY
SOUTHERN SEMINARY

I began to dig deeper into my memory of the Mahatma as the war's fury mounted. It was important, more than ever, to know the truth about the Mahatma, without understanding whom one cannot understand India. No man since the Buddha has won the hearts of the Indians so completely and symbolized their ethos so poignantly. Indeed there are other glittering figures in contemporary India, perhaps more appealing to Westerners, in a way, because of their own Westernism. Their Western symbols and English idiom are more understandable to the West, and they are, therefore, less disconcerting than Gandhi would be who is so uniquely Eastern. It may be that one or two of these Indian leaders might have imparted luster even to Western thought by sheer force of character and by the extra-Western information in their possession. But fundamentally these are the polishers of Western ways, although they were born in India. In sharp contrast, Gandhi represents what is distinctive of India. His contribution to the fast-developing global culture is, in consequence, also distinctive, and not merely an Easterner's endorsement of Western civilization.

The Mahatma will condition India even after he is dead. Maybe India will outgrow Gandhism in such fields as non-violence, industrialization, and birth control. But the new departures will be profoundly influenced by Gandhi's deeds and words. Both the government and private groups have produced daring plans for India's reconstruction along educational, medical, population, industrial, and agricultural lines, and none of these have been able to ignore Gandhi's influence, present or post-humous.

As the Wagnerian holocaust of World War II neared its climax, I saw Gandhi stand out as the most conspicuous challenge to a civilization to which wars are endemic because its core is competition. He stood at the other end of the pole from the modern and almost universal mood, so remote and so singular that his utterances at times sounded preposterous and his actions seemed maddening. But take him or leave him, Gandhi is Gandhi, cross-grained as a hickory knot. His actions were truly in the heroic tradition in as much as they calmly denied a global hysteria; but like the Mahatmas, or saints, of both the East and West in other centuries, his destiny was to be misunderstood.

Mahatmahood meets its Waterloo not only in the West. The best that can be said about India is that hers is the least hostile soil to the growth of a Gandhi. Her heritage provides a few more entrances and stage settings for a Mahatma; for her people can perceive grandeur of the spirit when they only half understand it. The East, with its reverential insensibility, lets its prophets die a natural death and does not exact martyrdom before deification.

Reading the writings of Gandhi and about Gandhi, besides imparting a sharp edge to my nostalgia for native ground, became an intellectual exercise to bring into focus the enigma of human striving versus determinism. I had lived in the West for more than a decade and steeped myself in what I considered was the best in her.

My Indian heritage was also tugging at the invisible cords of the subconscious. In my search for a philosophy of life in the atomic age, I vacillated between the West and the East, and Gandhi became to me the symbol of that un-geographic East which has not yet covered itself with the Western veneer. I felt that Gandhi was archaic in his biochemistry and in his physics, for philosophies, like pheasants, can be hung too long. But like Norman Cousins I also felt that modern man was obsolete in his insensitivity to universal unity and in his disregard of cosmic determinism in relation to free will. I was living amidst the dazzling successes of our machine civilization, which could not square up with the thousand little tragedies, mainly in the nature of psychological disturbances, of its individuals and groups. I could also recall the statistically staggering privations of my own people, which often hide real personal stability and happiness. I wondered whether a balance could be struck somewhere in between so that men, everywhere, would be modern and yet imbued with what Freud calls Oceanic Feeling.

I sought some guidance for my troubled intensity from Gandhi's autobiography, *The Story of My Experiments with Truth*, published in India more than two decades ago by the Navajivan Press, and the most revealing picture of the Mahatma's inner life up to 1920. As a high-school boy I had followed "the story" in Gujarati when it appeared in weekly installments in *Navajivan*, which Gandhi himself edited. Like the later autobiography of Nehru, it too was written in prison. When I read it again in American surroundings, I was struck by its observation of the removed fourth-wall convention of the Western theatre, in sharp contravention of the rules in Bharata's *Natyashastra* (the most influential treatise on Sanskrit dramaturgy) which prohibit even revealing one's back to one's audience. It read like a novel of adventure in spiritual jungles and though by no means a matrix of our age, it sounded like a fable for our time.

I looked into Gandhi's life from time to time as one looks into The Good Book, knowing full well that one is only too human to be able to follow The Good Book in its entirety. But the hope is this: A chance sentence might illuminate a disturbing problem; a familiar phrase might renew one's courage; an oft-quoted text might set one erect on one's path. Even when one cannot follow The Way, one may find new comfort and meaning in old and accepted truths. For great examples are like the lighthouse, repelling in a healthy way; it is dangerous to go near it but one may hold one's course by its radiance. Or, to take another nautical example, supreme artists of life can be likened to the North Star. Going east, west, or south, one can gauge one's position by its inexorable steadfastness.

The looking-inward that characterizes Gandhi's autobiography is bound to be the mood of my narrative also. Mine is a thinking-aloud book. In classical India, books which shared adventures in the realm of thought with their readers were always acceptable. Although in deadly earnest, these ancient authors often preferred to share their doubts rather than any conclusions with their readers. The classical Hindu writer behaved like a cogitator, improvising as if he were talking to you on a street corner, though using the written word. I know that such books are not in vogue in Europe and America in these days of political oracles and foreign correspondents who have the "real" story, and that is one reason why I want to call attention to the thinking-aloud vein of my book. I am still doubting, still uncertain as to which specific way will lead us to Utopia, nor do I quite know what comes more natural to human nature. But Gandhi travels a way which runs almost counter to the one taken by the so-called civilized world. And, knowing that we are approaching a dead end, it is plain good sense to find out where the other road leads.

Man's life is lived on two planes. Essentially all his activities and thoughts acquire meaning in terms of the two basic urges of his inner being. He marches, as it were, in two directions at the same time, and the more he is able to do so without conflict, the more he is integrated, happy. The ideal man of the scriptures is the one who has composed a unity of the two trends emanating from his life-motif.

One urge of life is horizontal. Man is born in a family, in a town, in a country, in a world, in collective history at a given moment. He thus becomes the social animal of Aristotelian definition. He is a part of community which in turn is given some of his qualities. Man must make his social equation with men, with his surroundings.

He must also make his personal equation with God, in whatever cosmic formula He is described or designated. For in addition to being a social animal, he is a solitude;

[xii]

man is alone. He is a child of eternity. This is the other impulse of life, the vertical impulse. It is experienced by each one of us in moments of grace, or inspiration, or of utter loneliness, and these moments occur more frequently with advancing years. And here the path is too narrow even for two persons; each individual solitude must tread an evolutionary course which would take it, not to the multitude—for that is realized by the horizontal trend—but to the existence eternal which some people call salvation. Solitude expands itself into the world-soul.

Vertical yearning dominates the horizontal in Gandhi. "My experiments in the political field," writes the Mahatma, "are now known, not only to India, but to a certain extent to the 'civilized' world. For me, they have not much value. . . . What I want to achieve—what I have been striving and pining to achieve these thirty years—is self-realization, to see God face to face, to attain moksha [salvation]." So his autobiography is vertical. It is not a tract on his time; it is the story of his "experiments with truth." His has been a life more independent of his time than that of any of his famous or infamous contemporaries. You can transplant his story into another age with very minor changes, and it will still sound credible. He conducts mass political movements according to the "voice of the conscience."

Add to the strange fascinations of his character the sheer story-book quality of his personality—diverting yet purposefully earnest; divinely maddening yet humanly contradictory; uplifting as a standard but inimitable and, therefore, repelling; charming and kind and joyous but severe at the center; so momentous and yet so unassuming. What he is, is at least as interesting as what he has done. On Gandhi's seventy-fifth birthday, Dr. Albert Einstein sent me a message to be used in a book I was editing, concluding: "Generations to come, it may be, will scarce believe that such a one as this ever in flesh and blood walked upon this earth."

Gandhi is a man of almost incredible contrasts. Gaunt, ascetic and self-denying, Gandhi is nevertheless the picture of health and agility. Nearing seventy-eight, Gandhi still retains a schoolboy complexion and radiance. He outwalks most youngsters during his daily strolls. His diet, although frugal, is scientifically planned and weighed, and his habits of living are as dependable as Big Ben. Recently Gandhi announced that not only does he expect to live to be 125, but that he will soon reveal his formula so that others can do likewise.

Like Thoreau he has ever been seeking a Walden, but his white-coated cabin has become "India's White House." Before a road was built and a telephone line (his only concession to modernism) installed, visitors and colleagues and foreign celebrities had to deal with miles of General Mud to reach Gandhi's hermitage. It is a simple affair of bamboos and mud, near Wardha, which is geographically to India what Emporia, Kansas, is to America. The round mound and the surrounding countryside were of rich soil, but without trees; the horizon was broken only by the sloping hills and jutting ridges.

The man who wanted to be alone is now surrounded

by a lively community and the headquarters of the various movements of which he has been a spearhead. Now there are orange and banana trees, and Persian wheels to bring water up from the parched earth. Three acres of land are covered with buildings of which only a few are made of brick and cement and tiles, and these are the offices of: the All-India Spinners Association; the All-India Village Industries Association; the All-India Anti-Untouchability League; and the All-India National Language Association.

There is a guest house, a school, and a post office, the humblest post office building in the world but, perhaps, one of the greatest in terms of the exchange of international correspondence.

Intensely devoted to causes, Gandhi has a keen sense of humor that never leaves him. He knows humanity's sorrow, and he also knows that sensitive souls should somehow manage to survive. "If I had no sense of humor," he confided once, "I should long ago have committed suicide." Being with Gandhi is like being at a party, and Gandhi is the life of a party.

But he is not a wit. His are not the calculated shafts of a sophisticate who knows how to get himself quoted. Neither is he what you would call clever. In fact, Gandhi's humor, so immensely enjoyed by people around him at the time, loses its quality in the retelling. You come away with the feeling that you have had a fabulous time, but you cannot reconstruct a humorous reminiscence from the experience. His laughter is contagious rather than memorable.

Mostly a spiritual gaiety, Gandhi's humor, once in a long while, turns to buoyant repartee, and this, for some reasons of his own, he reserves for his encounters with Westerners. There is the story of an English lady who was fascinated by the variety of fruit which had been sent to the Mahatma by his admirers in England. She exclaimed that she was prepared to be a saint if she could enjoy such delicious fare. Gandhi helpfully suggested, "You need not go so far to change your diet."

There was an American correspondent who asked: "Are you really a Mahatma?"

"I do not feel like one," was Gandhi's reply.

KRISHNALAL SHRIDHARANI

Contents

[xvii]

Contents

PART ONE: England, 1888-1891

"Listen to this!" shouted Monkey. "After all
the trouble we had getting here from China, and
after you specially ordered that we were to be
given the scriptures, Ananda and Kasyapa made a
fraudulent delivery of goods. They gave us blank
copies to take away; I ask you, what is the good
of that to us?"

"You needn't shout," said the Buddha smiling.
". . . As a matter of fact, it is such blank scrolls
as these that are the true scriptures."

—Wu Ch'eng-en

When Svetaketu was twelve years old he was
sent to a teacher, with whom he studied until
he was twenty-four. After learning all the Vedas,
he returned home full of conceit in the belief that
he was consummately well educated, and very
censorious.

His father said to him, "Svetaketu, my child,
you who are so full of your learning and so censorious, have you asked for that knowledge by
which we hear the unhearable, by which we perceive what cannot be perceived and know what
cannot be known?"

"What is that knowledge, sir?" asked Svetaketu.

His father replied, "As by knowing one lump
of clay all that is made of clay is known, the difference being only in name, but the truth being
that all is clay—so, my child, is that knowledge,
knowing which we know all."

—The Chandogya Upanishad

I. Three Vows

Don't aim to be an earthy Saint,
with eyes fixed on a star,
Just try to be the fellow that
your Mother thinks you are.
—Will S. Adkin

Iɴ Pᴏʀʙᴀɴᴅᴀʀ, a small Native State of Western India, on a sultry spring day in 1888, Mohandas Karamchand Gandhi, then a slender Hindu youth of eighteen, took three solemn oaths in the presence of Becharji Swami, the family priest.

"I shall not take to women.

"I shall not touch wine.

"I shall not eat meat."

Surrounding Gandhi in the small, incense-laden room were many members of his family and well-wishers who had come to witness a solemn ceremony, for Gandhi was the first of his caste-people to be planning to go to England, and by taking the three vows Gandhi hoped to gain the family's consent to his plans.

Putlibai, his saintly mother, had, at first, been unwilling to approve the realization of Gandhi's ambitious dream. In doubt, she had turned to Becharji Swami, a Jaina monk, who had originally been a member of the Bania caste to which the Gandhi family belonged.

The monk came to Gandhi's help and said, "I shall get the boy solemnly to take the three vows, and then he can be allowed to go."

When the oath had been administered, Gandhi's mother at last gave the youth permission to leave, and with the blessings of his elders, Gandhi started off for Bombay.

There was nothing unnatural about the mother's concern. She had heard that young men "got lost in England" and that they took to meat and liquor; these reports were deeply disturbing to a devout woman, who would not think of taking her meals without her daily prayers, and who for years had observed strict fasts despite illness.

The mother knew her son. It was not difficult for Gandhi to take these vows and to observe them faithfully. Gandhi had grown up in a religious and orderly household, with a solemn regard for truth and the utmost love for his mother and father. In his boyhood days he had been captivated by two plays, in one of which the theme was that of the hero's devotion to his parents, and in the other of which the hero was devoted to truth. These were ideals already alive in Gandhi's heart and, recalling the two plays fifty years later, Gandhi said, "For me, both [heroes] are living realities and I am sure I should be touched as before if I were to read again those plays today."

Three Vows

The first of his vows would undoubtedly be the easiest for Gandhi to observe. Married at the age of thirteen, he was devoted to his wife, Kasturbai. Describing himself as "passionately fond of her," Gandhi has revealed his early struggles with himself to gain control of the jealousy that tortured him soon after he was married. "I had absolutely no reason to suspect my wife's fidelity, but jealousy does not wait for reasons." But it was not long before he realized that his bitterness and severities were all based on love. "I wanted to make my wife an ideal wife. My ambition was to make her life a pure life, learn what I learnt, and identify her life and thought with mine." As for himself, Gandhi realized that "the passion for truth was innate in me, and to be false to her was therefore out of the question."

In all this, Gandhi has been typical of the orthodox Hindu. In India, the land of purdah, which has so carefully imprisoned sex, sexual relations, save for the procreation of children within the walls of wedlock, are considered unholy, immoral, and ugly. Morality in India has almost come to mean sexual morality. Except for professional prostitutes, the women of India are either virgins or married; nowhere else in the world is such a premium placed on virginity at marriage as in India. The eyes of the community are so trained to detect any irregularity that it can safely be said most extra-marital relations are with prostitutes.

The result has been that sex has an unusual fascination for Indians and yet that, as someone has said, the country is more starved sexually than nutritionally. It is not surprising that Gandhi speaks of the passion he had for his child-bride, that jealousy had been aroused in him at a tender age, and finally that he had already compelled himself to look deeply into his emotions, with the result that he had sworn lifelong faithfulness to his wife.

Drinking was not likely to be a problem for Gandhi. The overwhelming majority of people in India does not touch intoxicating drinks, and one can live and die in India without seeing a drunkard. Drinking is confined to the fashionable hotels and clubs, where Westernized Indians drink their chchota and buda pegs and their gin-slings. In a few large cities, such as Bombay, Calcutta, and Ahmedabad, industrial workers have taken to cheap liquor to escape and to forget their miseries. Religious literature discloses that the gods in heaven drink something that is named soma; and at rare religious ceremonies priests and laity alike partake of a deadly, if blessed, drink called bhung. The normal Hindu, however, has absolutely no taste for alcoholic beverages.

Even the third of Gandhi's vows, which friends had warned him might be impossible to observe in England, was readily undertaken. Gandhi came from a part of India dominated by the Jaina religion, which regards ahimsa, or non-violence, as "the greatest of religions." Jainas will not only refuse to touch meat, they also reject fish and eggs. They even make a distinction between higher and lower forms of vegetables, and some among them refuse to eat roots or anything that grows underground. They will not touch tomatoes because tomatoes are blood-red.

[6]

Three Vows

To a high-caste Hindu the renunciation of meat is not only a sign of refinement, but also a mark of spiritual growth. Hindus believe that there is a relationship between food and thinking, and that meat-eating fosters the passions. Meat-eating, they say, causes one to lose control of the senses, but, even more important, the taking of any life, be it that of fish or fowl or animal, to sustain one's own life, is an utterly degrading act.

Altogether, the demands that Putlibai had put upon her son were reasonable in the light of her religion and Hindu traditions, and Gandhi, one may be sure, took his vows without hesitation. Nevertheless, Gandhi became an outcaste, despite the permission of his mother and the blessings of the family priest.

When Gandhi reached Bombay, he was called before a general meeting of the caste and the Sheth, the headman of the community, said to him: "In the opinion of the caste, your proposal to go to England is not proper. Our religion forbids voyages abroad. We have also heard that it is not possible to live there without compromising our religion. One is obliged to eat and drink with Europeans!"

Gandhi replied that he did not agree with these views and that, in any event, he had made solemn promises to his mother "to abstain from three things you fear most."

This did not sway the Sheth, who pronounced his verdict: "This boy shall be treated as an outcaste from today. Whoever helps him or goes to see him off at the dock shall be punishable with a fine of one rupee four annas."

II. *True to Tradition*

So, with his brow he touched her feet, and bent
The farewell of fond eyes, unutterable,
Upon her sleeping face, still wet with tears;
And thrice around the bed in reverence,
As though it were an altar, softly stepped
With clasped hands laid upon his beating heart,
"For never," spake he, "lie I there again!"
And thrice he made to go, but thrice came back,
So strong her beauty was, so large his love:
Then, o'er his head drawing his cloth, he turned
And raised the purdah's edge:

—Sir Edwin Arnold

HINDU culture is strict about women, wine, and meat, but Gandhi himself has been far more severe. Though the father of four sons, Gandhi has been more opposed to sex than any religious leader in history. He has developed something of a mania on the subject. Not only is he opposed to passion on principle, he has also shown of late an utter disgust, a sense of horror, even for legitimate sexual relations. For Gandhi believes that true love between man and wife comes only after the conquest of carnal desire. The

[8]

great god Shiva, he recalls, took Parvati as his spouse after he had reduced Cupid to ashes.

In 1906, in South Africa, Gandhi, with his wife's consent, took a vow of brahmacharya, which means, literally, conduct that leads one to God; its technical meaning is self-restraint, particularly mastery over the sexual organs. He began to address Mrs. Gandhi as Ba, or Mother, while she called him Bapu, or Father. Speaking of the "glory of brahmacharya," and of "the freedom and joy" that came to him through chastity, he quotes the Bible of Hindus, *The Bhagavad Gita:* "The sense-objects turn away from an abstemious soul, leaving the relish behind. The relish also disappears with the realization of the Highest."

To become a member today of Gandhi's ashrama, or hermitage, one must take a vow of chastity. Husband and wife are permitted to live in the same house, but they are advised to sleep in separate rooms. Sometimes Gandhi has been known to have given a grudging consent to a marriage between two of his disciples, but he has seen to it that they do not have physical relations. To my personal knowledge he gave the following blessing to a bride who went to touch his feet, Indian fashion, shortly after the marriage ceremony: "Thou shalt have no children."

He admonishes the boys and girls of his ashrama not to meet in a room alone, or to exchange gifts. They may not enter the jungle for fear of lions. And Gandhi ascribes his ability for tireless work even during the twilight of his life to his years of brahmacharya.

[9]

A Freud might ascribe Gandhi's later feelings about sex to the fact that he was oversexed in his youth. Gandhi lifts the veil of mystery from his intimate relations with his child-bride in his autobiography, which is in some ways one of the most candid ever written. An incident that took place when he was sixteen provides a clue to his later asceticism. His father, to whom he was devoted as only an Indian son could be, was on his death-bed. Here are Gandhi's own words:

"Every night whilst my hands were massaging my father's legs, my mind was hovering about the bed-room —and that too at a time when religion, medical science and common sense alike forbade sexual intercourse. [His wife was expecting a baby.] I was always glad to be relieved from my duty, and went straight to the bed-room after doing obeisance to my father. . . .

"The dreadful night came. . . . It was 10:30 or 11:00 P.M. I was giving the massage. My uncle offered to relieve me. I was glad and went straight to the bed-room. My wife, poor thing, was fast asleep. But how could she sleep when I was there? I woke her up. In five or six minutes, however, the servant knocked at the door. I started with alarm. 'Get up,' he said, 'Father is very ill.' I knew of course that he was very ill, and so I guessed what 'very ill' meant at that moment. I sprang out of bed.

" 'What is the matter? Do tell me!'

" 'Father is no more.'

"So all was over! I had but to wring my hands. I felt deeply ashamed and miserable. I ran to my father's room. I saw, that if animal passion had not blinded me, I should have been spared the torture of separation from my father during his last moments. I should have been massaging him, and he would have died in my arms."

Something similar happened to Prince Gautama who became the Buddha. Something similar has happened to most saints of both the East and the West.

For a year during his high-school days, and long before he sailed for England, Gandhi was a meat-eater, but only because his "mind was bent on the 'reform.' It was not a question of pleasing the palate."

A wave of "reform" was sweeping the country. Schoolboys were singing:

> *Behold the mighty Englishman!*
> *He rules the Indian small,*
> *Because being a meat-eater*
> *He is five cubits tall.*

A school friend had persuaded Gandhi of the logic of the doggerel. His own elder brother had taken to meat-eating for the same purpose, but in secret, as the orthodox family would have been grievously offended. Some of his teachers were also reported to have surreptitiously joined the meat-eating fellowship.

More potent than the argument was the physical contrast that Gandhi felt in the presence of his meat-eating friend. The latter was much taller, stronger, could outrun Gandhi, and was the reputed hero of many an exploit. And young Gandhi wanted to be "strong and daring and wanted my countrymen also to be such, so that we might defeat the English and make India free."

"I had," wrote Gandhi of his first taste of goat's meat, "a very bad night afterwards. A horrible nightmare haunted me. Every time I dropped off to sleep it would seem as though a live goat were bleating inside me, and I would jump up full of remorse. But then I would remind myself that meat-eating was a duty and so become more cheerful."

The Hindu heritage reasserted itself and Gandhi "abjured meat out of the purity of my desire not to lie to my parents." Today Gandhi regards vegetarianism as one of the "priceless gifts of Hinduism," and by instinct and upbringing he has been trying for years to evolve a suitable vegetarian diet. Maintaining that the grosser the food, the grosser the body and mind, Gandhi denies that vegetarianism has made the Hindus weak. "We err in copying the lower animal world, if we are superior to it. For one thing the tremendous vested interests that have grown around the belief in animal food prevent the medical profession from approaching the question with complete detachment." He himself has adopted a simple diet of nuts and curd.

One of the invariable features of all Gandhi campaigns of civil disobedience has been the picketing of liquor stores and bars. Prohibition is such a concern with Gandhi that he did not hesitate, in 1937, when his National Congress Party came to power in the Provinces, to antagonize the Parsis of Bombay who held a sort of liquor monopoly and who had only lately responded to Gandhi's nationalism. "You will not be deceived," said Gandhi, "by the specious argument that India must not be made sober by compulsion. . . . In India . . . drink and drug habits are universally recognized as vice. Drink is not a fashion in India as it is in the West."

III. The English Days

A scientist says: Roast beef made England
what she is today. Moral: Eat more vegetables.
—Author unknown

Les grands mangeurs de viande sont en général
cruels et féroces plus que les autres hommes. . . .
La barbarie anglaise est connue.
—Rousseau

I<small>N</small> <small>AN</small> England full of
emancipated women young Gandhi arrived in October,
1888, with his vow that he would "not take to women."
In London, city of pubs, Gandhi came determined to
spurn even the friendly glass of ale. From a people
whose staple is boiled beef and mutton, Gandhi asked
vegetables and fruit. If Mr. Pickwick had been there to
observe the little Indian as he rushed toward the Inner
Temple, he would have indulgently put his hand on
Gandhi's shoulder and said with a twinkle in his eye,
"Sorry, lad, the best in us is barred to you."

The odds were definitely stacked against Gandhi
when he decided to live as an Indian in the latter-day

Rome. The Indian way of life is such that one can make social contacts on the street corner or in the village square. Or, sitting at the feet of a gaunt sage on the river bank, one may acquire a cultural understanding of India and probe into ancient philosophy and religion. In Western Europe and America the normal agencies of cultural exchange are the dinner table, the bar, and the ballroom. A club lounge is used as frequently as an office in making business deals. A woman-shunning vegetarian and teetotaler did not have a very good chance of being accepted, or of getting about, in the London of 1888.

Gandhi made gallant efforts, however. He landed on English soil in a white-flannel suit and was immediately made aware that he was the "only person wearing such clothes." He did not let many days pass before he acquired new clothes at the Army and Navy Store. Undertaking "the all too impossible task of becoming an English gentleman," he purchased an evening suit made in Bond Street, and a silk hat. He decided to take lessons in dancing but stopped with the sixth, as it was beyond him "to achieve anything like rhythmic motion." For a while he took lessons in violin playing to cultivate an ear for Western music, and he also tried to study elocution and French. But he soon decided it was a waste of time and money, that he was "pursuing a false ideal."

Thereafter, he seems to have spent most of his time at the business of being a vegetarian. Pages are devoted to the subject in his own story. He tells of the childlike thrill he experienced when he found a vegetarian restaurant in Farringdon Street, where he enjoyed the first hearty meal he had had since he reached London. He even devoured books on vegetarianism, such as Salt's *Plea for Vegetarianism*, Williams's *The Ethics of Diet*, Kingsford's *The Perfect Way in Diet*, and others. A friend suggested Bentham's *Theory of Utility* as an antidote, but he found it beyond his comprehension. His devotion to this cause, so un-English, won him the election to the Executive Committee of the Vegetarian Society, and he made his maiden speech in that capacity on the subject—of course—of vegetarianism. Though Gandhi was in England, he continued to tread the paths of India.

Busy as he was with his preparation for the London Matriculation and with his legal studies at the Inner Temple, he found time for those things in English life which were in harmony with his Hindu heritage. Other Indian students, such as Jawaharlal Nehru, who came to London much later, interested themselves in English politics, Western science, and international trade. But Gandhi was drawn to small and unrepresentative segments of English life, either because he was a misfit in the West building himself a protective shell of the familiar, or because, without realizing it, he was in revolt against the culture of England. In either case it was hard for him to adjust. He continued to wade in the tributaries, but he could not plunge into the Thames.

Toward the end of his second year in England, Gandhi came in contact with some Theosophists. They introduced him to *The Bhagavad Gita*, the essence of Hinduism, which was to become his guide for the rest of his life, and which, surprisingly, he had not yet read. Like many an Indian who has discovered his own land during his travels abroad, Gandhi found his religion in England. He read *The Bhagavad Gita* for the first time, not in Sanskrit, but in English, in Sir Edwin Arnold's eloquent translation entitled *The Song Celestial*. It gripped him instantaneously, especially the exhortation to self-control contained in the following lines:

> "*. . . If one*
> *Ponders on objects of the sense, there springs*
> *Attraction; from attraction grows desire,*
> *Desire flames to fierce passion, passion breeds*
> *Recklessness; then the memory—all betrayed—*
> *Lets noble purpose go, and saps the mind,*
> *Till purpose, mind, and man are all undone.*"

One day at a vegetarian boarding house, during a period when Gandhi was delving into books on Hinduism and Theosophy, a salesman sold him a copy of the Bible. He could not possibly read through the Old Testament, and the chapters following the Book of Genesis sent him to sleep. He disliked the Book of Numbers. "But the New Testament produced a different impression, especially the Sermon on the Mount which went straight to my heart."

It sounded like the Mahavira when he read, "But I say unto you, that ye resist not evil: but whosoever shall smite thee on thy right cheek, turn to him the other also." Here, on English soil, perhaps Gandhi found the first Christian confirmation of the Hindu idea which later blossomed into his fabled satyagraha, which has been mistakenly translated as passive resistance.

These pursuits deepened what was already within Gandhi by the way of cultural legacy, but it hardly helped him to understand Englishmen whose greatest adversary within the Empire he was destined to be. England, along with other countries of Europe and America, had adopted new values fostered by science and industry, values that were alien to the shy and serious young Hindu.

The authors and thinkers who appealed to Gandhi enough to be recalled in his reminiscences reveal it was not romantic, or new, or dramatic ideas that he was seeking or that held any spell for him. Instead, he seems to have been seeking and to have found affirmations—many of which came from unexpected directions—of his own cultural beliefs. These made a deep impression on his inverted personality. Ruskin, for example, became a part of him through his turning backward to agrarian culture and through his laments for industrial civilization. Later Gandhi translated Ruskin's *Unto This Last* in Gujarati, and became fond of *Crown of Wild Olives*. He read Plato and other founders of Western thought, but seldom mentioned them or quoted them, except that he translated Plato's *Apologia* and *Death of Socrates*. But that is understandable; for he was not so much impressed by Plato as by Plato's master. It was the absolute self-control and composure of Socrates—pointing to a path on which Gandhi was already embarked—that quickened him. He was later to prove that like Socrates he himself had a "daemon," and once that daemon had become "the voice of the conscience" and had been uttered, neither reasoning nor threats could sway him. Socrates, the exasperating goad of Athens, was given his cup of hemlock; Gandhi was sent to jail. The idea was the same. Gandhi's life has been a form of Greek tragedy in our time.

It was not Benjamin Franklin, to my mind one of the real architects as well as the rationalizer of "the American way," but Edward Carpenter who spoke to Gandhi from the New World. Gandhi also read Thoreau, and eventually breathed life into Thoreau's concept of "Civil Disobedience." He read other Boston Brahmins, whose New England "flowering" had turned out to be merely a table decoration in the mansion of America.

Among the European thinkers to make an impression on the growing Gandhi were, not Spengler or Marx, but Tolstoy. *The Kingdom of God Is Within You* led Gandhi to enter into a lively correspondence with the Russian genius. But there were two ideas which had crystallized, if not originated, in Europe that Gandhi made his own. One was nationalism; Gandhi devoured Mazzini. The other was democracy. Socially and philosophically prepared for it through centuries of traditions, the Hindu was grateful to observe political manifestations of democracy in the parliamentary institutions of England.

The knowledge of Latin that Gandhi acquired during his study of law in England furnished him the best bridge to the Western world—a mastery of simple, chaste, precise, and expressive English. The study of English law stood him in good stead when he launched his campaign against an excessively legalistic people.

Gandhi's stay in England ended abruptly and undramatically. He was called to the bar on the tenth of June, 1891; he enrolled in the High Court on the eleventh, and on the twelfth he sailed for home.

IV. The Native's Return

Superiority in India is a question of epidermis.
— Aldous Huxley

G ANDHI'S stay in India, after his return from England, turned out to be fairly brief, but it was an excessively difficult period in his life. First of all, there was the trouble with the caste that confronted him. Next, there was the desolating news of his mother's death, news which had been withheld from Gandhi while he was still in England. Gandhi writes of this severe blow, "My grief was even greater than over my father's death. Most of my cherished hopes were shattered."

Nevertheless, Gandhi immediately had to face the problems of coming into man's estate and of establishing a law practice. "My elder brother had built high hopes on me. The desire for wealth and name and fame was great in him." This did not make Gandhi's tasks any lighter.

The caste storm, which was still brewing, had divided the members of the community into two groups, one of

[21]

which was ready to accept Gandhi immediately into the fold, while the other was bent on keeping him out. To please the first group, Gandhi's brother found a swift solution. "My brother took me to Nasik before going to Rajkot, gave me a bath in the sacred river, and on reaching Rajkot, gave a caste-dinner. . . . The trouble about re-admission to the caste was thus practically over."

Gandhi never tried to seek admission to the section of the caste that had refused it to him, but by scrupulously respecting their feelings and regulations he was never thereafter troubled by that group.

The experience of "beginning life," of establishing a household, was full of pain and complications for Gandhi. The transition from the carefree life of a student to the practical everyday existence of making a living is trying in India, as anywhere else. According to the Hindu plan of life, Gandhi was now a grahastha, or a householder, with a duty to serve his clan; he was no longer a brahmachari, or student-celibate, to whom his clan owed support. The fact that Gandhi had not been a celibate during his student days reveals merely that many traditions which survive in a nation's culture are not necessarily carried out in practice; Gandhi's case was by no means exceptional.

There was an added problem for Gandhi. He was not simply an Indian turning from his studies to the business of earning his livelihood; he was a "returned-from-abroad" who once again had to conform to the ways of Hindu life. Although Gandhi's Anglicization was by no means so deep as that of many Indians who had been to

Britain and had elected to follow the ways of the rulers, it was there nonetheless. Gandhi, the reformer, had adopted some of the English ways, and these had to be reconciled with Indian ways. Moreover, he had to put his costly study of English law to advantage in his native land. Like every Indian who returns from studies abroad, though to a less intense degree, Gandhi was, for a time, a borderline case who belonged partly to two worlds but completely to neither, and who had to go through a process of harmonizing the two which can seldom be carried out to perfection.

At home in Rajkot, Gandhi's elder brother introduced English ways in anticipation of the young barrister's wishes. To this social pattern Gandhi added his own minor touches. Boots and shoes took the place of sandals, and harsh and angular European clothes took the place of the flowing and willowy tunics of India. Besides tea or coffee or cocoa, oatmeal porridge was added to the Kathiawadi breakfast of cream and wheat cakes.

All this meant added household expenses, especially as new things were added every day. "We had succeeded in tying a white elephant at our door. But how was the wherewithal to be found?" Gandhi asked himself. It was useless to think of starting practice in Rajkot and, after a short stay in his home town, Gandhi took the advice of friends and went to Bombay to gain experience in the High Court, study Indian law, and get what briefs he could.

In Bombay Gandhi set up a household for himself with a cook "as incompetent as myself." The cook was a Brahmin, for food cooked by a Brahmin, the highest caste, is acceptable to everyone, while food cooked by anyone of a lower caste cannot be touched. The result of this practice is, inevitably, that most cooks in orthodox India are Brahmins, while, for some inexplicable reason, most cooks in meat-eating families are Goanese whose culture has been shaped by Portuguese Catholicism.

Writing of this period, Gandhi vividly describes how he walked to and from the High Court, how he managed to do many household chores himself, how, in brief, he saved money. It seems that thriftiness was with him not only an art or a necessity or a desirable quality, but also an ethical principle. To be thrifty was to be good. It is an attitude most definitely ingrained in the Bania caste to which Gandhi belongs, and yet Banias are generally among the richest people in India, business being their business. It is an attitude that Frenchmen can appreciate, Englishmen can half grasp, and Americans cannot comprehend.

Even years later, when he was a full-fledged Mahatma, Gandhi used to clip the corners and edges of the newspapers given to him in Yeravda jail and write letters to his disciples on them. He could not bear the idea of using the jail stationery which had been purchased at the cost of Indian taxpayers. In the dining shed at his Sevagram establishment appeared a notice with Gandhi's signature: "I hope all will regard the property of the ashrama as belonging to themselves and to the poorest of the poor. Even salt should not be allowed to be served

in excess of one's needs. Water too may not be wasted."
He could not tolerate the extravagance of a mosquito
net, so he used to rub kerosene on his face before going
to bed to ward off visitations from the buzzing and
stinging insects which are even more numerous than
men in India. His economy is underlined with this virtue
of thriftiness. Instead of exhorting India to produce
more so that there will be enough to go around, Gandhi
teaches the doctrine of saving and of frugal living so
that there will be enough left to go around.

During this period of transition, the spiritual pursuit
of self-realization was poignantly evident in Gandhi's
life, and of course it never left him. Gandhi accepted the
Hindu theory that culture of the soul is difficult without
the aid and inspiration of a Guru, or master-teacher.
Sensing the truth in the doctrine that "true knowledge
is impossible without a Guru," Gandhi has searched
India for his Guru, but in vain. Gandhi never found a
person in the East or the West whom he could regard as
a Guru. I venture to suggest that Gurus are not for great
men whose illumination comes only from within. Men
like Gandhi are tortured souls who strive after perfection in their solitary ways, but eventually supreme tranquillity is theirs.

Meantime, Gandhi's efforts at legal practice in Bombay were not going so well. He had begun his study of
Indian law and his brother was trying his best to get
Gandhi briefs. Gandhi found the study of Indian law a
tedious business, and he was unnerved by stories of the
exploits of famous Indian barristers and vakils. Gandhi

felt he lacked the courage to conduct a case in court, and, in truth, he did, for he failed completely with the very first case that came his way.

It was, as Gandhi describes it, "a small cause" and "an easy case." Nevertheless, when Gandhi appeared in the Small Causes Court for the defendant, he found it quite impossible to cross-examine the plaintiff's witnesses. "I stood up, but my heart sank into my boots. My head was reeling. . . . I could think of no question to ask. . . . I sat down and told the agent that I could not conduct the case."

Adding to Gandhi's shame and confusion was his extreme embarrassment over the practice of paying commissions to "touts," pimps of the legal profession, who could bring him cases. He had steadfastly refused to pay a commission on his first case. Altogether Gandhi "found the barrister's profession a bad job—much show and little knowledge."

Throughout his two-year stay in India, he remained a "briefless barrister." But that was scarcely surprising. In India there are more barristers than ambulances, and most of them go without any practice to speak of for the first five years of their careers.

After "four or five months" of Bombay, Gandhi gave up the "bad job" and went back to Rajkot, there being no income "to square" with his ever-increasing expenditures.

About the chief thing he got out of his Bombay experience was what he called a little practical precept about living. "I hardly ever took a carriage or tramcar. I had

made it a rule to walk to the High Court. It took me
quite forty-five minutes, and of course I invariably returned home on foot. I had inured myself to the heat
of the sun. . . . When many of my friends in Bombay
used to fall ill, I do not remember having once had an
illness. . . . I am still reaping the benefits of that practice."

Back in Rajkot, a disappointed Gandhi set up his own
office, and he got along decently enough drafting appli-
cations and memorials. For his work he had his brother's
influence to thank but since this work came through the
settled business of his brother's partner, Gandhi once
again ran into the custom of paying commissions.
Deeply disturbed, Gandhi nonetheless had to compromise. The argument of his brother was, in the circumstances, unanswerable.

The work-a-day world around him was no less dis-
tressing. Rajkot is a peculiar town. It is a small British
Civil Station surrounded by scores of Western India
Native States, and is the headquarters of the British
Agent, who is an intermediary between the Maharajahs
and the Viceroy. It is, therefore, a center of intrigue
and of political maneuver. A hereditary prince of India
will go to great lengths to gain the favor of an English
clerk stationed in Rajkot. Diamond-studded, be-tur-
baned Maharajahs run obsequiously after the small fry
of the white community, at the same time showing dis-
courtesy to distinguished members of their own community. They may be seeking a reduction in their taxes,
or an increase in the number of ceremonial gun-salutes

allowed them, or an invitation to the Viceroy's tea. Things are changed drastically today, but in those days conditions made Gandhi sick at heart with the shame he felt for the slavishness of his own kind.

It was the inevitable atmosphere surrounding the Englishman in India. Imperialism is one part strength, two parts bluff, three parts exclusiveness, and four parts pomp. Lin Yutang says that Americans can never be good imperialists like the British because they like chop suey while the British disdain to eat it. Perhaps, in China, exclusiveness may have been the decisive factor in favor of English influence, but in India the English rule has exerted its force through "pomp and circumstance." During World War II, America's "top brass" in India might be seen to slap their Indian bearers on the back in true Rotarian spirit, but the Vicereine never deigned to bridge the distance between her car and her hair-dresser's shop in Delhi unless the royal red carpet had been spread before her. It was an English imperialist in India who gave Gandhi an experience that perhaps was a turning point in his life. "I got the first shock of my life," wrote Gandhi, "about this time. I had heard what a British officer was like, but up to now had never been face to face with one."

The British Political Agent at Rajkot was prejudiced against Gandhi's elder brother for what he conceived to be wrong counsel that had been given to a Maharajah. Now Gandhi had known this Englishman in England and had been fairly friendly with him there, so his brother persuaded him to go to see this Political Agent and try to put an end to the man's prejudice. Filled with pleasant recollections of their friendship in England, of the experiences they had shared there on terms of equality, Gandhi set out on his mission. Gandhi swiftly discovered the difference between India and England. There is a mystical and invisible line at the Suez Canal that most sensitive Indians who have traveled from East to West, or vice versa, have detected. Sailing from England, one suddenly finds, east of Suez, that one's English partner at table tennis or shuffleboard has failed to make his appearance; gone are the pleasant evenings of swapping highballs at the bar and singing together in the wee hours of the morning. Things are changed a lot now and the pattern of the new global community is slowly but unmistakably emerging, but this story of Gandhi's goes back to 1892.

Against his own judgement, Gandhi had sought an appointment to speak to the officer on his brother's behalf. But before he had had time to state his case, the Political Agent stood up with an I-have-no-time. When Gandhi said, "But please hear me out," the White Sahib ordered his peon to show the future Mahatma to the door. "I can scarcely have," recalls Gandhi, "taken up more than five minutes of his time. But he simply could not endure my talking. He could have politely asked me to go, but power had intoxicated him to an inordinate extent."

It seems Englishmen and Indians have more deplorably failed to meet on social ground than on political. It has been a caste problem between two countries extremely conscious of caste distinctions. When the British came to India, they brought with them not American ideas of leveling and standardization, but their feudal standards—to a country whose aristocracy antedates William the Norman.

Now, it happened that the Political Agent with whom Gandhi had had his encounter was also the magistrate in whose court most of Gandhi's work lay.

It was beyond Gandhi to conciliate him, and Gandhi was thoroughly depressed. His brother saw this, and both felt that Gandhi should find some job that would set him free from the atmosphere of intrigue at Rajkot. Gandhi was able to carry out a minor mission in Porbandar in connection with securing more powers for the Prince. "Even in this mission I was comparatively disappointed. I thought justice was not done to my clients but I had not the means to secure it. . . . Here the *sahib's* will was law. I was exasperated."

Fortunately, at this crucial turning point, Gandhi received an offer that changed everything for him and rescued him from the increasingly tormenting and unhappy round of his work in India.

V. Departure

*While Ananda was begging, he came to the
house of a prostitute named Maudenka who had
a beautiful daughter named Pchiti. This young
maiden was attracted by Ananda's youthful and
attractive person and pleaded earnestly with her
mother to conjure the young monk by the magic
spell of "bramanyika." This the mother did and
Ananda coming under the spell of its magic became fascinated by the charm of the young
maiden and entered the house and her room. . . .
The Lord Buddha had known all along what
was happening to Ananda and now called Manjusri and bade him repeat the Great Dharani at
the place where Ananda was yielding to temptation. As soon as Manjusri reached the house, the
magic spell lost its power and Ananda returned
to self-control.*

—The Surangama Sutra

THE opportunity came to
Gandhi through a group of Mohammedans who lived
in Porbandar, the town in which he had been born.
These Mohammedans had always been friendly to the
Gandhis, and the mutual interest between the two fam-

[31]

ilies, Hindu and Moslem, was true to the pattern of small-town India. There everyone belonged to the same community, and a Hindu boy of a small town will often call his elder Mohammedan neighbor "uncle," though no blood ties exist between them.

The Mohammedans had been doing a prosperous business for years in South Africa, and their firm was called Dada Abdulla and Company, with headquarters in Durban. They had a litigation pending in a South African court, involving $200,000, against an equally well-known rival firm of Indian Moslems doing business in Pretoria. The hometown boy, who hadn't yet made good but who had just returned with a glittering degree from the land of the rulers, was called in for consultation.

The man who built up the most fabulous income of any lawyer in South Africa, European or otherwise, was offered a first-class round-trip passage, the hospitality of the firm's South African representatives, and a fee of $525. He was hired merely as a minor adviser to the European lawyers already engaged in the suit. It was pointed out that he might also devote a couple of hours each day to taking care of the English correspondence of the firm.

"This was hardly going there as a barrister," Gandhi wrote. "It was going as a servant of the firm. But I wanted somehow to leave India." He closed "without any higgling" and got ready to go to South Africa. And Gandhi, who stayed in South Africa for eight years, emerging as the strong and recognized leader of Indian expatriates, the man who changed the whole pattern of white-brown relationship in a landscape drawn up in black and white, assured his wife that he would return in a year—to stay.

Arriving in Bombay, Gandhi had difficulty securing passage, but he was able to make arrangements at the last moment. The particular boat on which he wanted to travel had no first-class berth available, and the captain had offered him the spare one in his own cabin. On the trip, the captain, keen on chess, saw in Gandhi not only a playmate but also an apt pupil, and the Englishman and the Indian became fast friends and inseparable. This friendship had one dire consequence for Gandhi some days later, or as Gandhi puts it, "The Captain liked me much but the liking took an undesirable turn."

When the ship docked at Zanzibar, the captain invited another Englishman and Gandhi to what he termed "an outing." Not knowing what "an outing" meant, Gandhi merrily went along, to find himself suddenly in a Negro woman's quarters.

"Little did the Captain know what an ignoramus I was in such matters. . . . We were each shown into a room. I simply stood there dumb with shame. Heaven only knows what the poor woman must have thought of me. . . . This in my life was the third trial of its kind. Many a youth, innocent at first, must have been drawn into sin by a false sense of shame."

When finally the English captain's voice boomed outside, Gandhi "came out just as I had gone in," and

Gandhi "thanked God that the sight of the woman had not moved me in the least. I was disgusted at my weakness and pitied myself for not having had the courage to refuse to go into the room. . . . I could claim no credit for having come out unscathed. . . . The incident increased my faith in God and taught me, to a certain extent, to cast off false shame."

When Gandhi learned that the ship was to remain in port for a week, he decided to take rooms in the town, and wandering about he saw sights that impressed him. "Only Malabar can give any idea of the luxuriant vegetation of Zanzibar." The ship's next stop was Mozambique, and from there it went on to Natal, where Gandhi landed toward the end of May, 1893.

PART TWO: South Africa, 1893-1914

Having offered himself as a sacrifice, Nachiketas surprised Death and entered the abode of Death where there was no one to receive him.

After an absence of three nights Death returned, and said, "O Brahmin, as thou, a venerable guest, hast dwelt in my house three nights without eating, therefore choose now three boons."

. . . The third time Nachitekas said, "There is doubt when a man is dead—some saying, he is; others, he is not. This I should like to know taught by Death himself; this is the third of my boons."

Death said, "Take sons and grandsons, all long-lived, cattle and horses, elephants and gold, take a great kingdom.

"Anything but this. Wealth, long life, Nachiketas! empire, anything whatever; satisfy the heart's desire.

"Pleasure beyond human reach, fine women with carriages, their musical instruments; go beyond dreams; enjoy. But do not ask what lies beyond me who am Death."

Nachitekas said, "Destroyer of man! These things pass. Joy ends enjoyment, the longest life is short. Keep the horses, keep singing and dancing, keep it all for yourself.

"What man, subject to death and decay, getting the chance of undecaying life, would still enjoy mere long life, thinking of copulation and beauty.

"Say where man goes after you claim him. . . . This, which you have made so mysterious, is the only gift I will take." *—The Katha Upanishad*

VI. An Honest Lawyer

*If the advocate refuses to defend from what
he may think of the charge or of the defense, he
assumes the character of the judge; nay, he assumes it before the hour of judgement; and, in
proportion to his rank and reputation, puts the
heavy influence of, perhaps, a mistaken opinion
into the scale against the accused.*

—Thomas Erskine

*The law of God, which we call the moral Law,
must be the scope, and rule, and end, of all laws.*

—John Calvin

A FEW days after his ar-
rival in Durban, the Port of Natal, Gandhi created an
incident. On this first of his working days in South
Africa, Gandhi was taken by Abdulla Sheth, head of
the firm, to the Durban court to be introduced to various people. Gandhi was seated next to Abdulla Sheth's
lawyer and soon realized that the magistrate was staring
at him. Finally, the magistrate asked Gandhi to take off
his turban, but Gandhi refused to do this and had to
leave the court.

Now, just as it is customary for a Westerner to remove his hat in a courtroom, it is equally natural for an
Indian to keep his turban on. A turban, or any type of
Indian headgear, is not merely a protection against the
sun and the wind and the rain; it is a sign of respect for
the person you are meeting or the place you are visiting.
It shows that you are properly dressed.

Costumes in South Africa, however, did not bear out
the caste requirements of India; they followed, instead,
the pattern of the African caste system imposed by the
ruling Boer-British alliance. Most of the Indians in South
Africa were laborers and were called "coolies." To
avoid that classification, Moslem merchants claimed to
be "Arabs" and thus retained the privilege of keeping
their turbans on. Hindu merchants also claimed to be
Arabs in order to avoid unnecessary embarrassments,
while the Parsi clerks claimed to be Persians—Indians
were anything but Indian. Despite all these evasions,
sooner or later every Indian was bound to be called a
coolie.

Gandhi, refusing to take off his turban and walking
out of the court, did the equivalent of writing a "letter
to the *Times*." It provoked wide discussion, even Europeans dividing themselves pro and con on the question
of the "coolie barrister" who had earned for himself
such premature notoriety.

For the first few days, Abdulla Sheth thought Gandhi
to be a white elephant saddled with the howdah of an
English degree and indefensible notions of human equality. Illiterate but wise, he took to talking Islam to the

Hindu, and Gandhi learned a great deal about the teachings of the Prophet. When the time came to send Gandhi to Pretoria to look after the case, Gandhi frightened his host and employer by saying, "I . . . intend cultivating the acquaintance of the other party. . . . I would try, if possible, to settle the case out of court."

Abdulla Sheth could not believe his ears. "Yes, I see. But [our opponent] is not a man to consent to a settlement easily. . . . Please think twice before you do anything."

When Gandhi reached Pretoria and talked to the attorney in charge, Baker by name, he found that another expensive counsel had already been hired, and that all that was required of him was to act as a liaison man between the lawyers and Dada Abdulla, transmitting the progress of the case to the client. Baker was far more interested in talking Christianity to the Hindu lawyer whom he believed certain to fail of going to heaven unless he "accepted Jesus as the Saviour."

Gandhi started to study the case on his own, and in time became convinced that he knew the facts better than anyone else. In his leisure time he acquired prestige among the Indians of Pretoria by organizing meetings for civic purposes. Meanwhile he had formed a friendship with Tyeb Sheth, the defendant, in spite of the warnings his own client had given him. Finally, when, on the basis of the study of all the facts, he was convinced of the justness of his client's claim, he persuaded both sides that the continuance of the litigation would ruin both of them financially and that the honorable course was one of arbitration. Moreover, he was not content even when his client won. He felt that "his duty was to befriend both the parties," and he went out of his way to secure for his defeated opponent a plan of payment based on moderate installments—a plan which would prevent bankruptcy. He acted as a lawyer for both sides.

Disgusted with lawyers who dug up additional points of law which inevitably prolong legal proceedings and increase ill-will between the litigants, and ashamed of those belonging to his profession who merely sought larger fees, Gandhi came to the conclusion "that the true function of a lawyer was to unite parties riven asunder." It became a part of his philosophy of law. A large part of his time during twenty years of legal practice was, consequently, spent in bringing about private compromises of hundreds of cases. He saved his soul, and he lost nothing, "not even money." In fact, his practice flourished along with his ardor for honesty.

A great help came to him from his knowledge of the Hindu Law, considered by historians to be the oldest legal system. Two main characteristics of the Hindu Law, now fast disappearing under the impact of legal institutions established by the British, have a direct bearing on Gandhi's understanding of the true function of law in society. To Hindus, law was personal and hereditary. A Punjabi took his own law along with him when he settled down in Bengal. A Brahmin had a slightly different code of social obligations from that of a Shudra. Secondly, Hindu tribunals were private tribunals. An offense was judged at the different levels that might be affected—by the family tribunal, by the trade or profession tribunal, by the caste tribunal, or by the community tribunal. In this way the directness of human relationship was prevented, as far as possible, from becoming stylized or impersonalized by cut-and-dried application of abstract controls and sanctions.

His case finished, Gandhi's mission to South Africa came to an end. He very much wanted to go back to India, but prominent members of the Indian community persuaded him to stay on in order to help ease the sufferings of his countrymen at the hands of the Union Government and the white community in general. He decided to stay on. He refused, however, to live on public funds even while performing public service, and resolved to earn his living as a lawyer.

Settling down in Natal, he presently applied to the Supreme Court for admission as an advocate. In doing so, he tossed a bombshell—all hell broke loose. The Law Society of Natal had never heard of such a thing. Gandhi might be acceptable enough personally, but no colored man had ever dared before to aspire to such a status. Once colored people were admitted to the Bar, would not they flood the legal profession and drive out the whites? They staunchly opposed Gandhi's application, and applied devious measures to meet the brown man's threat to a country which was, for all they cared, white and was to remain white in spite of the fact that ninety-five per cent of the population was Negroid. But the Coolie Barrister who was reaching for the stars—

this first non-European to apply for admission to the South African Supreme Court—was receiving a great deal of publicity to boot, and liberal individuals as well as a united press were supporting his case.

"The law makes no distinction between white and colored people," announced the Chief Justice of the Supreme Court of Natal, when Gandhi's application came up for official review. Justice, it appeared, was indeed blind and, therefore, unable to judge a person by the color of his skin. Gandhi was asked to stand and take the oath. A bit of history was made.

Shortly Gandhi acquired fame as "honest Gandhi." He refused to take a case until he had studied all the facts and satisfied himself that his client had a just cause. In doing so, he forced himself to sacrifice huge sums and excellent chances, but he would not argue in support of a doubtful claim, let alone a trumped-up one.

On one occasion, an Indian caught in the act of smuggling goods ashore without paying duty and who was threatened with a severe prison term, appealed to Gandhi to save him. All that Gandhi thought he could do in the matter was to bring about a settlement short of imprisonment. Gandhi took the case and as usual went through his client's books. Unfortunately, the books recorded that the defendant had previously smuggled in much more than the customs officer had realized. Gandhi actually compelled his client to confess all to the customs officer, won the latter's approbation, and brought about a compromise. "I was confirmed in my conviction," observed Gandhi, "that it was not impossible to practice law without compromising truth."

Once he was trying a case in Johannesburg. He had studied all the facts submitted to him and had come to the conclusion that his client was right. But in court, Gandhi saw, his client was breaking down under the fire of the opposing lawyer's cross-examination. In an instant he realized that his client had falsified the facts on which the defense was built. Disgusted with his deceit, and conscious of his duty, he rose to interrupt the proceedings.

"Your Honor, I move that the case of my client be dismissed without any argument," requested Gandhi.

There was a stir in the audience, and the judge was visibly moved by Gandhi's candor. He publicly approved Gandhi's conduct, praised his integrity, and dismissed the case. Conscious-stricken, the man begged Gandhi's pardon for having involved him in the "shady" affair. Gandhi was pacified, and judges and juries in South Africa from that time on were aware that Gandhi would never consciously defend any dubious claim, however attractive the reward.

It would be misleading to suppose that Gandhi was fully supported on all sides. Many famous jurists, at the time and subsequently, have taken issue with the Mahatma. On the grounds of professional ethics, they have challenged Gandhi's attitude. The first loyalty of a lawyer, they argue, is to his client who has given to him a sacred trust. The client seeks defense, protection, vindication, and it is to provide these that a lawyer is hired. To let him down for personal, moral, self-righteous reasons is, they feel, a breach of the lawyer's code. They contend that a client is more important than a conscience in court.

Yet it is these very "professional" duties of a lawyer that Gandhi considers "immoral." To side with clients rather than with truth, to ferret out arguments in favor of clients instead of in the interest of justice, Gandhi holds, are evils of a profession which has become too civilized and is now divorced from its original purpose.

Law should be a harmonizer of the individual and collective trends. But the growing complexities of civilization has made it, in Roscoe Pound's words, a form of "social control through the systematic application of force of politically organized society." The obligations of the individual are ritualized and imposed by the society through law. Here collectivity supersedes individuality. Not only are individual freedoms endangered, but individual moral obligations are relaxed until they touch the law. A habit of mind is engendered whereby a remedy for evil is found in a fresh law. As the French jurist Dalloy has pointed out, "Each fresh law being a fresh miscalculation, men are continually led to demand from it what can proceed only from themselves, from their own education and their own morality." A millionaire has no moral scruples about evicting a pauper from a tenement house; he has the legal right to do so. The impersonal austerity of law has freed men from the human considerations which arise out of intimate human contacts.

In this manner, law, which was laid down to govern

the moral behavior of man, becomes an inspiration for unethical actions, immorality. This is a tragedy, perhaps inevitable, of the complex modern societies wherein direct or face-to-face relations have become fewer and fewer and indirect legal relations have multiplied. We live by symbols and ignore the truths they represent. We conform to formalities and forget about the human needs to serve which those formalities were created. Busy with living, we accept all this, but an artist of life —and Gandhi is one—rebels against these expressions of truth which conceal the truth. Preoccupied with eternity and not lost among social customs and prevailing habits of mind, Gandhi has an irrepressible urge to go deep—into the meaning of life.

Salvador de Madariaga thinks that Gandhi, more than a man of action or a man of thought, is "a man of life." There are two ways of insuring anything—authority and example. The former is an organizational and objective process. The latter is subjective on both sides, between the teacher who does not teach and the taught, between the giver who does not give and the receiver. It is the more difficult process of conveying meanings, but it conveys a living sense of realities as only life can. And if the permanent problem of human communities is the adjustment of collective and individual trends, emerging in different forms in different ages, then the Gandhian method of example, which is prophetic and in India traditional, is more suited to man's needs and of more enduring worth.

VII. Colored Traveler

Little Indian, Sioux or Crow
Little Frosty Eskimo,
Little Turk or Japanee,
Oh, don't you wish that you were me?
　　　　　　　　　　—R. L. Stevenson

A man who is not an Aryan is betrayed by
behavior unworthy of an Aryan: harshness, cru-
elty, and neglect of duty.
　　　　　　　　　　—The Code of Manu

LONG before Gandhi established himself as a lawyer and public figure in South Africa, in fact as soon as he had landed, he had suffered, along with the rest of his countrymen, countless indignities and cruelties at the hands of the all-powerful white man.

Just a week after he had arrived, Gandhi sat huddled, shivering, in a dingy, chilly waiting-room at Maritzburg, capital of Natal. It was as cold as a winter night in the high regions of South Africa could be. Gandhi was too numb and too confused to make an effort to secure his overcoat from his luggage—the torment in his heart was overwhelming. Suppose he were to ask the station authorities for his luggage and be insulted again. No, he hadn't the strength left in him to try it.

Over and over again, Gandhi reconstructed in his mind the sad experience that was torturing him. He had left Durban that morning for Pretoria to take charge of the case of his client. Impeccably dressed in a European suit, he had taken his first class berth on the train as the Indians of Durban were wishing him godspeed. He had taken off his turban and made himself comfortable, and read documents pertaining to his case.

About nine o'clock that night the train stopped at Maritzburg, and there had been some coming and going in other compartments but not in his, for he was traveling first class. Suddenly, however, the door opened, and in came a passenger. He looked Gandhi over, decided that he was colored, and out he went. He returned with two railway officials.

"Come along, you must go to the van compartment," said one of the officials to Gandhi.

"But I have a first class ticket," said Gandhi.

"That doesn't matter," said the other official. "You must go to the van compartment."

"I tell you, I was permitted to travel in this compartment at Durban, and I insist on going on with it," Gandhi replied.

"No you won't," said the official. "You must leave . . . else I shall have to call a police constable to push you out."

"You may. I refuse to get out voluntarily."

[47]

The constable came in. Without a word he threw Gandhi's bags on the platform, took the little man's hand, and pushed him out. The railway authorities took charge of his luggage, except for a handbag Gandhi carried.

In the station, Gandhi had no fire, no food, but he had plenty of time to mull over his misery. He recalled that from the first he had seen Indians being frequently insulted by the white population of South Africa. They lived in restricted areas, and they were denied the acquisition of property elsewhere. Theirs was a ghetto existence. Or were the untouchables' quarters of India a closer analogy! Time after time Gandhi had noticed that he himself was less impudently treated because of his dress, his education, his manners. But again and again he had also shared the same humiliations. Now had come the crowning act.

Should he go back to India and leave this country where Indians, Chinese, and certainly the native Negroes, were not treated as equal human beings? Should he return to Durban, his case unfinished, and sail on the first boat? He was torn, about to make a decision that was to change the relations between man and man, and especially between the Asiatic and the Westerner.

A European approached him at midnight as Gandhi sat there ruminating, brooding, vacillating, but Gandhi had no desire to talk, no wish to be insulted again. He wanted to be left alone in his misery. Again he started his mental debate. Should he fight for his rights or go back to India? Should he go on to Pretoria not minding the insults and return to India after the case was finished? Would it be cowardice to hurry home to India without carrying out his obligations? Was the hardship a surface thing—a symptom of some deep disease? Should he try to root out the disease and suffer hardships in the process?

Gandhi decided to stay. To fight. His mind at peace, he planned to take the next train to Pretoria.

He was met in the morning by Indian merchants who had heard of his mission and its unhappy interruption. They had come to take him home and look after him. They tried to console him by saying that each of them had gone through similar experiences and that there was nothing to be done about it. All day long, Gandhi listened to their tales of woe, and gritted his teeth. The meek was aroused.

In the evening word came that the railway company had reserved a first class berth for him on the next train if he cared to proceed to Pretoria. He took it. You cannot fight all your battles from one trench.

The train did not go beyond Charlestown. In those days, a stage-coach completed the journey to Johannesburg. The white man in charge of the stage-coach, known as the "leader," decided that Gandhi could not sit inside with European passengers. A "coolie" must take whatever comes. Gandhi "pocketed" the insult and sat in the leader's place outside while the former moved inside.

Near Pardekoph, the leader felt like having a smoke, and also a breath of fresh air, as the inside of the coach was stuffy. So he came out, spread a piece of dirty sack-cloth on the footboard, and turned to Gandhi, "Swami, you sit on this. I want to sit near the driver."

"It was you who seated me here, though I should have been accommodated inside. I put up with the insult. Now that you want to sit outside and smoke, you would have me sit at your feet." And Gandhi added, "I will not do so, but I am prepared to sit inside."

The strong man went for the weak and began to box his ears. Then suddenly in a rage of temper, he seized the brown man and tried to drag him down. Gandhi, silent and determined, clung to the brass rails of the coach-box. He decided that he would risk breaking his wristbones rather than let this bully have his way.

The group inside was watching the strange drama. One man was tall and white, the other brown and short. One man was powerful as a teamster, the other fragile as a clerk. One man was storming and shouting; the other received the abuse in silence but showed a determination that warmed the onlookers' hearts.

"Let him alone," a cry rose from the passengers inside the coach. "He is not to blame. If he can't stay there, let him come and sit with us."

The leader was crestfallen. His own kind had let him down. He let Gandhi go, but swore at him again and vowed he would get even. Then he kicked the Hottentot servant who was sitting on the other side of the coach-box, asked him to sit on the footboard, and took the seat thus vacated.

At Standerton, Gandhi asked the cabbie to be driven

to the Grand National Hotel. The manager looked him over and said politely, "I am very sorry, we are full up."

When Gandhi told this to his Indian hosts in the town, they laughed knowingly, like old hands, and told him that South Africa was not a country for such as he. They nodded their heads, and related their experiences. Gandhi again made firm resolves.

They also told Gandhi that conditions in Transvaal were much worse than in Natal. Here, the authorities never sold first class or second class tickets to Indians. One had to travel third or stay at home.

Gandhi, determined to travel first class, decided to present himself at the station "in faultless English dress" and "possibly" persuade the station master to sell him a first class ticket.

The station master was moved to pity. He smiled. "I am not a Transvaaler. I am a Hollander," he said. "I appreciate your feelings. . . . I do want to give you a ticket—on one condition, however . . . you will not involve me in the affair." With this he gave Gandhi the ticket.

The Indians who had come to see Gandhi off were surprised at Gandhi's success in securing the first class ticket, but they prayed that their precious barrister would reach Pretoria without broken bones.

It happened at Germiston. A guard came to examine the tickets. He was beside himself when he found a colored man in the first class compartment. He began to shout and to order Gandhi out. An English passenger in the compartment came to Gandhi's rescue. Turning to the guard, he said, "What do you mean by troubling the gentleman? Don't you see he has a first class ticket? I do not mind in the least his traveling with me."

"If you want to travel with a coolie, what do I care?" grumbled the guard and he went away.

About eight in the evening, Gandhi reached Pretoria. It was the journey's end for the Coolie Barrister. But it was only the beginning—of the long road he had set out to travel.

VIII. Behind God's Back

Thou shalt neither vex a stranger, nor oppress him: for ye were strangers in the land of Egypt.
—Exodus

THE Indian problem in South Africa, or the South African problem in India—it all depended on one's viewpoint—was older than Gandhi. It began nine years before Gandhi was born, on November 16, 1860, when the first group of indentured laborers from India landed at Port Natal.

The English, who had settled in Natal, and who had obtained land concessions from the Zulus by every conceivable means, needed cheap labor to work their plantations. Slavery had been abolished by then, so that they could not coerce the Negroes to hard labor. Nor could the natives be coaxed into it. The Zulu was accustomed to an easy life; it was not difficult for him to take care of his yearly necessities through six months of work on the land and in the jungle.

The English settlers in Natal approached the English rulers of India, played upon their sympathies and common ties, and invented a new form of slavery which

[53]

differed from the old in so far as it was not lifelong but was year-marked. The Indian government agreed, largely out of consideration for their fellow Englishmen bent upon making fortunes in the Dark Continent, to supply cheap labor under terms of indenture. Certain economic protections were provided for the Indians, but no civic rights, let alone civil liberties.

Lured by the European planters of Natal and the mine-owners who—like the early settlers of the North American colonies—hoped to develop the country, and encouraged by the Indian agents of South African industrialists, the Indians came as indentured laborers under five-year contracts. They were brought over in lots, having been put under contract before they left India.

At the end of the five years of contract labor, the more aggressive and enterprising among them began to set up shop in the strange land, instead of returning home. Some of them started small business concerns, and others acquired small plots of land which presently they turned into truck farms. Gradually they began to compete with the white trash, if not with the very people who had used their physical energies for five years. In their wake came many educated Indians, free of indenture, to handle their affairs, particularly their retail businesses, and the ranks of these, in turn, were swelled by Indian lawyers and doctors. By 1894, there were approximately 60,000 indentured, 10,000 ex-indentured, and 10,000 "free" Indians in Natal alone, in comparison with 400,000 Zulus and 40,000 Europeans. By 1906, Transvaal had 12,000 more.

The European community reacted according to custom. It forgot that the Indians had come at its own invitation. It also forgot the contribution of the Indian labor in the development of mines and plantations. Now that there was no particular further use or need for such labors, the whites sought to harass the Indians out of South Africa. The expatriates were badgered, robbed, threatened.

Over and above this illegal persecution of Indians, the Europeans began to prepare legal avenues for their eviction. They drew up bills that would force every indentured laborer, at the expiration of his contract, to pack up and leave. In 1906, the government of Transvaal introduced a bill in the legislature which, upon its passage, would require every Indian to be registered by fingerprints. It would also require him, like a criminal, to produce his certificate of registration upon the demand of any policeman at any time. Delinquents were to be deported.

Indians had known many hardships before. They had put up with many insults. But in this bill they saw the beginning of the end of the Indian colony in South Africa. They protested against the bill's passage. They sent deputations. They met in mass meetings and passed resolutions. They agitated. They wrote letters to the editors. But nothing came of it all, and the government went ahead and passed the bill, an act which the Indians felt to be an affront not only to themselves but also to their race and nationality. They wondered what would happen next; with them, also wondering, was Gandhi.

IX. Satyagraha Is Born!

With folded arms and steady eyes,
And little fear, and less surprise,
Look upon them as they slay,
Till their rage has died away.
Then they will return with shame
To the place from which they came,
And the blood thus shed will speak
In hot blushes on their cheek.
                              —Shelley

THE old Empire Theatre was packed from wall to wall on September 11, 1906. Delegates from Indian communities all over Transvaal had come to attend the fateful meeting. There were Indian merchant princes among them, and indentured laborers—half slaves. There were farmers and shopkeepers and lawyers and doctors, and there was also a sprinkling of women clad in saffron and pink saris. Various political organizations that Gandhi had been able to establish in South Africa in so brief a stay were also represented there. And in the front row sat reporters from the South African press, visibly amused at the show these berobed "Swamis" and illiterate "coolies"

[56]

were staging. But among them also sat a serious-looking Indian reporter, representing *Indian Opinion,* a new paper which Gandhi had started and which was flourishing not only among Indians, but also among Europeans who were intrigued by the future Mahatma's extraordinary views.

Sitting on the dais, surrounded by the stalwarts of the Indian community, Gandhi "read in every face the expectation of something strange to be done or to happen." Nobody was quite sure what it was all about, save that the Union Government was out to annihilate them and that they should meet the peril, somehow, like men.

Someone was saying, "If I am asked to give my fingerprints and produce my registration certificate, I will shoot the man and then end my own my life."

Another man was suggesting, "The best thing is for all of us to pack and go home, en masse, and leave this God-forsaken country to those who would have it. Where will they get cheap labor? How will they fill in the gap in their commercial life created by our departure?"

Still another one was pleading, "We should send one deputation to India and another to England."

An impatient bearded Sikh was shouting, "We should get hold of whatever weapons we can find, and fight like men."

Gandhi was conscious of such views, which formed the background of the fiery speeches being delivered from the dais. The tension rose as the speeches progressed. Every one of them was eager to do something, to show his mettle somehow, but nobody knew just what to do, or how to do it. The known weapons of violence were not for them; they subconsciously feared the use of them, knowing their opponent was far more skilled in handling them. Like the Legions of Right in the old epic *Mahabharata*, they were mutely praying to God to rend the sky and throw down to His people a new weapon which would stupefy their antagonist.

Gandhi rose. There was no more whispering. They were hushed, choking with expectation, as they looked upon the young barrister who was championing their cause. Without realizing what he was doing, Gandhi announced, "I, for one, would refuse to obey the Black Ordinance and take the consequences—go to jail, if need be, or die."

The atmosphere was charged with they knew not what. People were on their feet, feeling for the first time that there was something that they could do. The Moslem chairman of the meeting suggested that each person present should take the same oath in the presence of God!

That brought home to Gandhi a sense of what he had done, a sense of immense responsibility. It slowly dawned on him that this resolution, unlike all the others that had been passed previously, was not aimed at any effect upon people outside the meeting hall. This was meant to steel their own souls, to instill the idea that the battle lay within. And if even Gandhi did not at first know its full implications, how could others have done so? He rose again, to explain, as he records in *Satyagraha in South Africa:*

"Everyone must only search his own heart, and if the inner voice assures him that he has the requisite strength to carry him through, then only should he pledge himself and then only would his pledge bear fruit. . . . We might have to go to jail, where we might be insulted. We might have to go hungry and suffer extreme heat or cold. Hard labor might be imposed upon us. We might be flogged by rude warders. We might be fined heavily and our property might be attached and held up to auction if there are only a few resisters left. Opulent today we might be reduced to abject poverty tomorrow. We might be deported. Suffering from starvation and similar hardships in jail, some of us might fall ill and even die."

Each person present took the oath to resist unto death the Black Ordinance. But they were to resist not by inflicting suffering on their enemy, but by inviting suffering on themselves, as a price for their disobedience. Submit not to evil, and take the consequences, was the central theme. Gandhi, and a few others, knew that a new weapon was born. It put power, as it were, in reverse. Power is created somewhere in between the one who imposes his will and the other who accepts it. By refusing to submit to the tyrant's will, his power is destroyed. It was a sort of jiu-jitsu tactic wherein you unbalanced the charging opponent by getting out of his way.

[59]

LIBRARY
SOUTHERN SEMINARY

The meeting broke up, and everyone went his way, not only to resist the Black Ordinance, but also to secure new signatures from those who had not been present when Gandhi spoke. In no time most of the Indians, including the women and children, were pledged to offer the type of resistance Gandhi had suggested. And as the movement progressed, Gandhi searched his brain to find a name for his new weapon and to formulate its theory and practice.

Gandhi had many friends among the Anglo-Saxons and Boers; there are always enlightened souls, who are ready to go against the majority of their own kind when they feel that justice is at stake. One of these was Mr. Hosken, a tycoon of Johannesburg. While introducing Gandhi to a gathering of sympathetic Europeans, he described the movement in the following terms: "The Transvaal Indians have had recourse to passive resistance when all other means of securing redress proved to be of no avail. They do not enjoy franchise. Numerically, they are only a few. They are weak and have no arms. Therefore they have taken to passive resistance, which is a weapon of the weak." These well-meant remarks, broad attempts of a Westerner trying to understand the new movement in terms of Western history, shook Gandhi from his intellectual slumber. Was his struggle to be misunderstood because there was no better name for it than "passive resistance?" The term was being used in connection with the great suffragist movement in England. The suffragists had no vote, and they were weak indeed, but they did not eschew the use of physical force. They set buildings on fire and assaulted people. But there was no place for brute force in the Indian movement. Another English example of passive resistance was that of the Nonconformists who, under the leadership of Dr. Clifford, passively resisted the Education Act. They were indeed weak in numbers, but Mother India had millions of sons. Gandhi rejected the concept of "passive resistance."

His weapon had roots in Indian heritage. The ancient Vedas had a philosophy of suffering that brought divine as well as worldly results. Suffering, self-imposed and undergone in the spirit of grace, was an instrument of self-purification, and self-purification led to victory on a higher plane or even the highest. Most of our wrongs arise not only out of the oppressor, but also from the oppressed. The tyrant has the power to impose only that which the victim lacks the strength to resist. To discard our own weakness and wickedness is, therefore, half the battle, and that is the way of suffering and self-purification. It is impossible, however, to achieve this without granting the innate goodness of human nature, the unity of mankind, and the all-embracing power of love.

In the Western world, too, Gandhi's idea of suffering had a firm foundation. The motif of suffering is central to Christianity. The Cross still moves multitudes through its symbolism of the most magnificent suffering in history. It stirs emotions that remain untouched by argument and by reasoning. The Church won a triumph over the Roman Empire, not through persuasion nor through power, but through suffering and martyrdom.

It is no wonder, then, that Gandhi should go back again and again, as he does to *The Bhagavad Gita*, to the Sermon on the Mount. And there is a touch of pathos or irony to remember that this weapon founded on forgiveness was propounded in a Jewish theatre in South Africa. Gandhi persuaded his countrymen, most of whom were Moslems, to discard the Semitic doctrine of an eye for an eye, a tooth for a tooth.

Some of Gandhi's Western friends wondered whether what he taught was in conformity with the dignity of the individual. When the individual is assaulted, they argued, the final recourse he has to protect his dignity is to hit back. By failing to do so he proves to be unworthy of himself, a coward. But Gandhi answered that it requires greater courage to remain mentally and spiritually unyielding under the pressure of blows. To refuse to strike back and, at the same time, to refuse to submit is the height of dignity. To feel that the bully deprives one of one's dignity by physical abuse is to admit that one entrusts one's dignity to an outsider. Fundamental human dignity is part of one's character, and character cannot be changed by mere physical pressure. His weapon, therefore, was not for the cowards and weaklings, claimed Gandhi. Were it a choice between cowardice and violence, he would prefer violence. More courageous than violence, argued Gandhi, was non-violence.

As the movement progressed in South Africa, Gandhi hit upon the idea of naming his new weapon of resistance Satyagraha. Satya means Truth in Sanskrit and implies love, while Agraha means firmness which engenders force; they combine to say, "The Force which is born of Truth and Love or Non-Violence." He also described it as "soul force" for those who found it difficult to pronounce the Sanskrit compound.

Borrowing the phrase of Henry David Thoreau of Walden, the New England recluse who fought against slavery by refusing to pay taxes to a government which practiced slavery, Gandhi called the particular stratagem of Satyagraha which he was employing against the South African government "civil disobedience." Only those who are otherwise willing to obey the law, insisted Gandhi, could have a right to practice civil disobedience against unjust laws. It was quite different from the behavior of outlaws, for it was to be practiced openly and after ample notice. It was not likely, therefore, to foster a habit of law-breaking or to create an atmosphere of anarchy. And it was to be resorted to only when all other peaceful means, such as petitions and negotiations and arbitration, had failed to redress the wrong. There was in it something that recalled the American Frontier, where people took the law in their own hands when both the sheriff and the magistrate had been found corrupt and Washington was too far away.

Later on, in India, Satyagraha evolved into an intricate strategy of non-violent direct action which differs from war in so far as the latter is violent direct action. It includes such strategems as agitation, demonstrations, negotiations, and the seeking of arbitration. Then come such economic measures as sanctions, strikes, picketing, the general strike, commercial boycott, and sitdown strikes. Non-payment of taxes is another method of thwarting the powers that rule. The instrument of non-cooperation is less known in the West, but its power has been adequately displayed in South Africa and India. "Even the most despotic government," Gandhi says, "cannot stand except for the consent of the governed which consent is often forcibly procured by the despot. Immediately the subject ceases to fear the despotic force, his power is gone." The means of ostracism is an Indian equivalent of the labor unions' treatment of "scabs." And finally there is the instrument of starting a parallel government.

But it has been Gandhi's frequent hunger strikes that have held the West most particularly spellbound. The technique of self-starvation is not of Gandhi's own making. It was called sitting dhurna in olden days. Every so often in the Middle Ages a moneylender, failing to receive his money back in due time, would sit at the gate of the house of the defaulter, refusing to budge from his place or to take any food until the client paid in full. Since the interesting situation always gathered a crowd, the debtor would make a supreme effort to pay rather than suffer a long drawn-out siege with its attendant embarrassment. The Bhat, or royal bard, used a similar method when he wanted his king to "be a man" and fight. When his ruler, out of cowardice or other considerations, refused to meet an invading or offending king in combat, the Bhat would sit at the palace gate and start a hunger strike. In most cases, this compelled the king to fight. Here the principle of suffering and the purifying influence of vicarious suffering on the feelings of others was involved. It had the same ennobling effect which, according to Aristotle, high tragedy has.

An Englishman would naturally find it difficult to imagine the Leader of His Majesty's Loyal Opposition going on a hunger strike to convince the Prime Minister of his errors. An American cannot visualize the Minority Leader in the Senate going on a fast unto death to get a bill approved. Harder still is it to envision a John L. Lewis refusing to touch food until a raise was insured for his miners. And yet there have been significant examples of the same phenomenon in the Western world. The hunger strike of the Lord Mayor of Cork, which resulted in his death in prison during the Irish Home Rule Movement, was one such example. There was another instance of a similar nature during the American Revolution. Commenting on the significance of June 1, 1774, when the Port of Boston was to be closed by the British, Thomas Jefferson wrote: "We were under the conviction of the necessity of arousing our people from the lethargy into which they had fallen as to passing events; and thought that the appointment of a day of general fasting and prayer would be most likely to call up and alarm their attention. . . . We cooked up a resolution . . . for appointing . . . a day of fasting, humiliation and prayer, to implore heaven to avert from us the evils of civil war, to inspire us with firmness in support of our rights, and to turn the hearts of the King and Parliament to moderation and justice.

"The people met generally, with anxiety and alarm in their countenance, and the effect of the day through the whole colony was like a shock of electricity, arousing every man and placing him erect and solidly on his center."

X. *The Mahatma and the Marshal*

Be careful in dealing with a man who cares nothing for sensual pleasures, nothing for comfort or praise or promotion, but is simply determined to do what he believes to be right. He is a dangerous and uncomfortable enemy because his body which you can always conquer gives you so little purchase over his soul.

—Gilbert Murray

The scent of flowers does not travel against the wind, nor that of sandal-wood, or of Tagara and Mallika flowers; but the fragrance of good people travels even against the wind; a good man pervades every place.

—The Dhammapada

GANDHI's person was not safe after he launched his campaign in South Africa. Once on one of his daily strolls he approached President Kruger's house, unaware that no colored man was allowed to do this. Before he knew what had hit him, he was pushed and kicked into the street by a guard on duty in front of Kruger's residence.

Before Gandhi could speak, a friend and fellow lawyer, an English Quaker by the name of Coates, arrived upon the scene. He hurried over to Gandhi and exclaimed, "Gandhi, I have seen everything. I shall gladly be your witness in court if you proceed against the man. I am very sorry you have been so rudely assaulted."

Gandhi told his friend that he need not be sorry. Turning toward the policeman, he said, "What does the poor man know? . . . I have made it a rule not to go to court in respect of any personal grievance. So I do not intend to proceed against him."

The guard apologized to him, and, as Gandhi says, "There was no need. I had already forgiven him."

In 1896, after a hasty trip to India to enlist the mother country's help in his fight for Indian expatriates in South Africa, Gandhi was set upon by a crowd in Natal. They encircled him and showered him with bricks, stones and rotten eggs. Had it not been for the courage of the wife of the police superintendent, who happened to be passing by and who immediately went to Gandhi's aid, the incident may well have had a grave ending. Nevertheless, when the then Secretary of State for the Colonies, Mr. Chamberlain, cabled the Natal Government to prosecute Gandhi's assailants, Gandhi wrote back: "I do not want to prosecute anyone. . . . I am sure that when the truth becomes known, they will be sorry for their conduct."

Lasting over a period of eight years, the Indian movement in South Africa entailed untold suffering for Gandhi's men, and unending discomfiture for the Union Government. When the Indians resorted to the civil

disobedience of the Black Act, the administration
struck back with imprisonments, convictions, and fines.
Eventually Gandhi was arrested. But droves of Indians
continued to follow Gandhi, overflowing jails, and thus
paralyzing one coercive agency of the state. The constant struggle, moreover, kept the issue alive and prevented the law from being carried out. The European-
in-the-street was becoming more and more aware of the
injustice involved in the daily suffering so courageously
and passively endured by the Indians. How often does
man practice injustice only when he can get away with
it—and also when he can forget it immediately afterwards! The Indians were not letting the South Africans
forget it, and they were gradually succeeding in breaking down the moral defenses of the opponents. Forced
by an aroused public opinion, General Smuts, then
Prime Minister but not yet Field Marshal, visited
Gandhi in jail and undertook to have the law repealed
if the Indians would register of their own accord.

The Indians agreed and did their part. The Prime
Minister, however, broke his promise, and the Transvaal
Government passed even more stringent laws. In 1913,
a decision of the South African Supreme Court invali-
dated all Hindu and Mohammedan marriages, thus rendering all Indian children illegitimate and consequently
debarred from inheriting the property of their parents.
Again Gandhi took up his struggle.

Indians by law were forbidden to pass from Transvaal
to Natal. Defying the injunction, Gandhi led a procession of Indian women across the border and started a

[69]

vigorous picketing of the Natal mines. The matrons were arrested and incarcerated in due course. When this news became known, some five thousand Indian miners came out on strike. Controlling their fury, they started a march back to Transvaal on foot, a long line of stalwarts who sang patriotic and religious songs as they followed tiny Gandhi in this strange spectacle. En route, Gandhi was arrested three times and released as many times, but the miners kept their walking vigil, maintaining their own discipline. All of them were imprisoned, some of them were beaten and wounded. But they held their peace and lifted not a finger in retaliation. The news reached India, and even the British Viceroy, Lord Hardinge, defended the Satyagrahis and scored the Union Government in a public speech. By and large, the South African Government was receiving a bad press all over the world. It was in a delicate position anyway, because a strike had broken out among the European railwaymen.

At this juncture, Gandhi came out with one of the master strokes of Satyagrahic strategy. Instead of taking advantage of this two-fold crisis of the Union Government, Gandhi chivalrously suspended the Indian struggle until the administration had settled with the European railwaymen. The government fully appreciated Gandhi's help and many Europeans, who had hitherto been hostile, expressed admiration for the fair play Gandhi had shown.

Concrete results followed immediately. Prime Minister Smuts yielded at last. Every important demand of the

Indians was granted. The fingerprint registration was abolished, the three-pound head tax was repealed, and Hindu as well as Moslem marriages became valid once more in South Africa. The restriction on the immigration of educated Indians was lifted, and the government promised to protect the rights of the Indians by a just administration of existing laws.

Years later, on the occasion of Gandhi's seventieth birthday, Field Marshal Smuts paid the following tribute to the Mahatma: "It is fitting that I, as an opponent of Gandhi a generation ago, should now salute the veteran as he reaches the scriptural limits of three score years and ten. May the further allotment which the Psalmist grudgingly allows also be his, and may they be years of fruitful service to the world and of a peaceful mind to himself! . . . I must frankly admit that his activities at that time were very trying to me. Together with other South African leaders I was then busily engaged on the task of welding the old colonies into a unified state. . . . Suddenly, in the midst of all these engrossing preoccupations, Gandhi raised a most troublesome issue. We had a skeleton in our cupboard in the form of what is called the Indian question in South Africa. . . . Gandhi tackled this problem, and in doing so showed a new technique—one which he afterwards made world-famous in his political campaigns in India. . . . Large numbers of Indians had to be imprisoned for lawless behavior, and Gandhi himself received—what no doubt he desired—a short period of rest and quiet in gaol. For him everything went according to plan. For me—the defender of law and order—there was the usual trying situation, the odium of carrying out a law which had not strong public support, and finally the discomfiture when the law had to be repealed. For him it was a successful coup. Nor was the personal touch wanting, for nothing in Gandhi's procedure is without a peculiar personal touch. In gaol he had prepared for me a very useful pair of sandals which he presented to me when he was set free! I have worn these sandals for many a summer since then, even though I may feel that I am not worthy to stand in the shoes of so great a man!"

Gandhi's was a weapon which could make such a spiritual and deep understanding possible between two men who had fought each other, the Mahatma and the Marshal. Many Indians have been proud of their culture for using a weapon that is without hatred and rancor in situations which might otherwise lead to bloodshed. Many Englishmen have perceived a tribute to their own race and to their own tradition of fair play in Gandhi's application of so Christian a weapon against them, instead of the customary violence. Englishmen, it is interesting to observe, contend that non-violence can work only against themselves, for they conform to the rules of the game; they feel it would be impotent against ruthless dictators. Gandhi has taken every occasion to pay tribute to the British character, but has also pointed out that the very chivalry of his weapon tends to invoke reciprocal chivalry among his opponents. Man cannot help but be good, Gandhi believes, if he is appealed to on moral grounds.

XI. Is the Hindu a Heathen?

I am praying to be lighted from within, and
not simply to hold a light in my hand.
                                        —Tagore

Behold but One in all things; it is the second
that leads you astray.
                                        —Kabir

These rivers, my son, run, the eastern toward
the east, the western toward the west. They go
from sea to sea. They become indeed sea. And
those rivers, when they are in the sea, do not
know, I am this or that river.
                        —The Chchandogya Upanishad

THE more Gandhi became
entangled in concrete problems of world leadership, the
more deeply he searched into the reaches of the soul. His
preoccupation was that of the spiritual and moral perfection of self, so that he could continue his striving
toward the ideal through this life, as he must have done
through past lives, until at last he came to the final unity
which is achieved in godhead. The usual goal of man in
the West is to advance oneself materially, to promote

oneself in a career or job, to secure a place in society, to love and to be loved and respected by one's fellow men, to earn enough to give security to one's family. The general aim in India is to use this life as a stepping stone toward life everlasting, and Gandhi symbolizes that urge more than most Indians.

His beatific behavior attracted many Christian enthusiasts in South Africa, and his own ethical endeavors landed him amidst Christian struggles. There began a race to save the heathen Gandhi by converting him to Christianity. Gandhi's mind was open, but he asked to be shown the light.

A fellow lawyer, A. W. Baker of the case which had brought him to South Africa, led Gandhi to his own private prayer meeting. A group of devout Christians kneeled down, somewhat in the manner of the Salvation Army, and prayed for the brown man who had knelt with them out of courtesy: "Lord, show the path to the new brother, who has come amongst us. Give him, Lord, the peace that Thou hast given us. May the Lord Jesus who has saved us save him too. We ask all this in the name of Jesus."

Another lawyer, Mr. Coates, who had figured in the incident at President Kruger's residence, gave Gandhi books on Christianity, and took evening walks with him in the hope that the heathen would see the light through his discourses. Gandhi faithfully kept a diary of what he had read and what impression his readings and conversations had made on him. This he regularly submitted to Coates for his comment each time they met.

Is the Hindu a Heathen?

Once Coates noticed around Gandhi's neck a necklace of Tulasi-beads, and promptly decided it was evidence of Hindu superstition. He said to Gandhi, "This superstition does not become you. Come, let me break the necklace."

"No. . . . It is a sacred gift from my mother," countered Gandhi.

"But do you believe in it?"

"I do not think I should come to harm if I did not wear it. But I cannot, without sufficient reason, give up a necklace that she put round my neck out of love. . . . When, with the passage of time, it wears away, I shall have no desire to get a new one."

Coates was convinced that Gandhi could not be saved until he embraced Christianity, which represented *the* truth. So he introduced the heathen to a family of Plymouth Brethren.

One of them took Gandhi by surprise by saying: "You must be brooding over your transgressions every moment of your life, always mending them and atoning for them. How can this ceaseless cycle of action bring you redemption? . . . How can we bear the burden of sin? We can but throw it on Jesus."

To this Gandhi replied: "I do not seek redemption from the consequences of my sin. I seek to be redeemed from sin itself, or rather from the very thought of sin. Until I have attained that end, I shall be content to be restless." The Law of Karma was speaking, in the terms of which life is a process of becoming, through the deeds that you do and do not perform. Grace is not bestowed

by someone, however divine, outside of you. It is a state
of mind that you achieve through your own strivings.

But the Plymouth Brother pointed out that man must
sin, that it was impossible to live in this world sinless,
and it was for this that Jesus suffered and made atonement. And Gandhi notes that "the Brother proved as
good as his word. He voluntarily committed transgressions, and showed me that he was undisturbed by
thought of them."

While reporting this to Coates the Quaker, Gandhi
anticipated his rejoinder, and said he knew that "all
Christians did not believe in such a theory of atonement."

Baker, meanwhile, was getting anxious about Gandhi's
future, so he took the latter to a revival meeting of
Protestants. The atmosphere of religious exaltation and
physical frenzy, he thought, would sweep Gandhi off
his feet and bring him into the fold of the Church.

Baker soon realized that his companion was not only
a man to be saved by Christianity but a colored man. He
had the courage of his faith, however, and succeeded in
persuading his fellow Christians that Gandhi was acceptable in the eyes of God, though not quite white.
For three days and three nights those assembled Christians prayed for Gandhi, but that simple soul could find
no reason to change his religion.

Once C. F. Andrews, one of Gandhi's most devoted
Christian friends, and one of the few persons who came
closest to the Hindu's definition of a Christian, invited
Gandhi to a church because he was going to preach the

sermon. Busy as he was, Gandhi went late instead of accompanying Andrews. The guards at the church gate stopped the colored man. In good humor, and smiling at the absurd situation, Gandhi waited by the wayside, hoping to walk back home together with his friend, who lived with him.

Coming out of the church, Andrews rebuked Gandhi. "You promised to come and listen to me. And you failed me."

"But the guards at the church entrance would not let me in," Gandhi protested.

"They would not let you into the church, and your gospel of love was the text of my sermon!" Andrews murmured half to himself.

What troubled Gandhi about formal Christianity was: "It was more than I could believe, that Jesus was the only incarnate son of God, and that only he who believed in Him would have everlasting life. If God could have sons, all of us were his sons. If Jesus was like God, or God Himself, then all men were like God and could be God Himself."

Truth or God is one in Hinduism. But there could be various ways of approaching Truth or realizing God. Like the center of a circle, it can be reached on a myriad axes from the periphery. The idea of *the* way, or *the* Prophet, or *the* gospel sounds rigid and exclusive to a Hindu who is more a philosopher than a church-goer. Gandhi also felt that all living beings had souls, while Christian doctrine grants souls only to human beings. The picture of a Buddha saving the lives also of lambs was more touching to him than the picture of Jesus healing only human beings.

As Gandhi was unwilling to accept the superiority of Christianity, he was equally unconcerned about establishing the superiority of Hinduism. "Hindu defects were pressingly visible to me. . . . What was the meaning of saying that the Vedas were the inspired Word of God? If they were inspired, why not also the Bible and the Koran?"

All sages of India, without exception, have sung that God is One who is known by a myriad names. The idea of changing religious labels in order to secure spiritual blessedness is, therefore, abhorrent to them. Hinduism is perhaps the only great religion which never believed in an evangelical missionary movement. One should share the richness of one's experience with fellow men, but one need not insist that inner growth is impossible without change in outer allegiances. The best way to help a Hindu is to make him a better Hindu, just as the best way to help a Christian is to make him a better Christian.

The Indian's peculiar dislike of conversion is also born of political experience. Rightly or wrongly he has felt that throughout the East, in the past, missionaries have been the outriders of imperialism. Even today, no American missionary is permitted by the British to enter India until he signs a written pledge "to do nothing to, or in diminution of, the lawfully constituted authority of the country." The doctrine of rendering unto Caesar that which is his is not appealing to a people who believes that everything is God's. And the very notion of evangelism expresses an impulse of self-righteousness. Moreover, the spectacle of mass conversion, often seen in the West, is strange and incredible to a Hindu. It is impossible, he feels, for five thousand persons to hear the voices of their consciences at the same time, the phenomenon of associational reverie notwithstanding. Rice religion only enhances the corroding influence of a safety-first, security-first civilization.

A group of statesmen of Christianity traveled up to Gandhi's Sevagram headquarters to spend a few days with the Mahatma in 1938. One of them asked whether Gandhi would not concede the possibility of a real conversion on occasion. To this Gandhi readily agreed, but he added that a missionary's life should be like a rose's. Let him lead an exemplary life amidst his community, and let the witnesses discover its fragrance of their own accord, and try to follow the example of the missionary if they so choose. Then John R. Mott inquired whether Gandhi was not pleased with the new turn the missionary movement had taken of recent years. The Mahatma replied that he thought very little of a religion that had to be supported by millions of dollars.

Turning to John S. Hoyland, he added: "I think that you cannot serve God and Mammon both, and my fear is that Mammon has been sent to serve India and God has remained behind, with the result that He will one day have His vengeance. . . . I have always felt that when a religious organization has more money than it requires, it is in peril of losing its faith in God, and pinning its faith on money. You have simply to cease to depend on it."

Gandhi, however, has "remained forever indebted" to those early Christian friends who tried to convert him, for the religious quest that they awakened in him. As a result, he learned the truths of Christianity. He read the Koran. He studied the teachings of Zarathustra in the original and not through Nietzsche's interpolations. He went through Jewish theology and drank the honey of Confucius's wisdom. In his daily living he profited by gathering truths from whatever direction they came, teaching his followers to be students of comparative religion and respecters of all faiths.

Particularly he came to appreciate the poetry and inspiration of Jesus's death on the Cross, and visitors have noticed that in his tiny thatched hut there is only one picture—that of the Man of Nazareth.

A NOTE ON HORIZONTAL RELIGION

The bursting of the atom bomb should quicken the quest of a global faith such as Gandhi exemplifies in his life.

One unmistakable thread in recent thinking on the crisis of our age, which has twice exploded in world wars within the memory of most living men, is that scientific pluralism and relativity of intellectual approach have rendered impotent most of the moral controls born of religious belief, and thus given a freer reign to men's and nations' passions.

[80]

Is the Hindu a Heathen?

At the same time, developments in technology, especially in the fields of transportation and communication, have produced the phenomenon of a shrunken world wherein yesterday's total strangers have become today's next-door neighbors. Different groups and cultures are consequently thrown together in a world of interdependent living.

But the world of the spirit has not witnessed any similar progress which would have prepared the minds of men for the physical world revolutionized by science. This has been described by some as cultural lag.

If these basic assumptions are true, then it follows that moral controls born of religious belief must be revived in order to ensure peace. And granting the necessity of global approach in affairs of men in the shrunken world of ours, we should see to it that the revived ethical controls are universally applicable and based upon religious principles acceptable to all mankind. Scientific universalism has given us scientific humanism, a system lacking the driving power of religious belief. To provide bridges for cultural understanding, a global system of religious belief is clearly called for.

And yet it must be conceded that all historic attempts at establishing a universal religion have themselves resulted in bloody wars. The conflict between the Crescent and the Cross, resulting in the Crusades, is only the best known example. It will be clearly irreligious to provide a religious basis for world peace by waging another set of religious wars. Bridges are needed, not trajectories.

A study of historic religious conflicts shows that contending religions shared almost similar sets of moral principles although they differed violently in their respective theologies. Similarly, present-day peace among the various religions is underlined by a common universe of ethical values stemming from various theological systems.

It is easy to see, then, that it is possible to unite all great religions in a universal system of ethics, since all of them uphold similar commandments of human conduct. What is lacking is an official blessing.

As pointed out before, man's life is carried on through two fundamental drives. One drive is horizontal, embracing his living on this earth with other men during a specific period of time. The other drive is vertical, aimed at the final equation of his individual soul with the cosmic reality described variously by various religions.

This distinction is recognized by most great religions. In Western philosophy, the distinction between natural law and the revealed law is made in recognition of the two planes on which the individual functions.

A world religious congress should not find it impossible, therefore, to evolve a global ethical creed based upon the natural law systems of various great religions. Theology should be left entirely out of consideration except in places where it claims exclusiveness capable of producing intolerance in the horizontal behavior of men.

The questions may be raised whether this new global ethical creed will be as sterile as scientific humanism; whether it will lack the appeal to action that only religion can make; whether it will have the emotional fervor of a religious pursuit.

I contend that since the universalism of the new ethical creed will be based upon the various religions, it will have the emotional appeal of the religious phenomenon. What we shall be trying to evolve is a universal system deriving its inspiration from various theologies. We would be achieving horizontal harmony in a universe of distinctive vertical approaches.

Nothing can be more universally inspiring and cohesive than a new world religion. But like the San Francisco Charter, horizontal unity is the best we can get from advocates governed by their distinctive theologies. And once we have this global philosophy capable of inducing religious fervor, I suspect that it will redound on an eventual world religion satisfying the needs of all peoples.

The time is ripe. If we believe anthropologists and ethnologists, the prime cause of primitive religions was fear, fear of man's unknown origin and of the dark unknowable end. But today we are not so much afraid of our ancestors or of our future in heaven or hell as we are of our fellow men. We are fearful of our very life in this atomic age. In stark contrast to the primitive men who were vertically afraid, we of today stand in awe of the new horizontal fear unleashed with the energy of atoms. What we need is a horizontal religion, the religion of man. Gandhi has given the world a shining example.

[83]

PART THREE: India, 1915-1944

Then the Blessed One spoke and said: "Know, Vasetha, that from time to time a Tathagata is born into the world, a fully Enlightened One, blessed and worthy, abounding in wisdom and goodness, happy with knowledge of the worlds, unsurpassed as a guide to erring mortals, a teacher of gods and men, a Blessed Buddha. He thoroughly understands this universe, as though he saw it face to face. . . . The Truth does he proclaim both in its letter and in its spirit, lovely in its origin, lovely in its progress, lovely in its consummation. A higher life doth he make known in all its purity and in all its perfectness.

—*The Tevigga Sutta*

When not enlightened, Buddhas are no other than ordinary beings; when there is enlightenment, ordinary beings at once turn into Buddhas.

—*Hui Neng*

XII. The Year of Silence

Think not silence the wisdom of fools; but, if rightly timed, the honor of wise men, who have not the infirmity, but the virtue of taciturnity.
—Thomas Browne

Silence is audible to all men, at all times, in all places.
—H. D. Thoreau

IN THE second week of January, 1915, a slim, short, and dark Indian came down the gangplank at the Apollo Bunder, within sight of the stark, impressive marble Gateway of India through which Viceroys had entered and departed from their domain. It was a native's return after years of achievement overseas. The unmerciful Indian sun beat down upon the Parsi Towers of Silence, the domes of the Hindu Temple in Girgaum, the minarets of the Moslem Mosque in Bhindi Bazaar, and the nearby Bombay Yacht Club of English colonials with serene detachment and impartiality. Contradicting the saying that only Englishmen and mad dogs venture out in the noonday sun, a vast crowd filled the harbor with life.

[87]

Forty-six years old but looking younger, and clad in a shirt and dhoti under his Kathiavadi cloak which was overlaid with a decorative sash, Gandhi looked "somewhat more civilized than I do now." As he reached the soil from which he had sprung, he was astounded. All he had expected to meet was a handful of politicians in sympathy with the cause he had so valiantly and successfully championed in South Africa. He saw, instead, a surge of Bombay's humanity, a teeming multitude whose imagination he had caught from across the ocean.

Two things had especially touched his compatriots. He had enunciated a doctrine of non-violence which had revived in the collective consciousness of India's millions the image of Gautama the Buddha. Their traditional fountainheads of emotion had been stirred as they had not been for two thousand years. They were more devout than curious in their regard for the frail man whose only weapon against a strong adversary had been love.

Gandhi's sacrifices and asceticism had also gripped them. Son of the prime minister of a Native State, and the most renowned advocate before the South African Bar, Gandhi had given away his all, and had taken vows of poverty and service. In America it is success which inspires admiration and respect. In India it is renunciation that captivates the hearts of men.

Moreover, from his political laboratory in South Africa, an ocean away, Gandhi had arrested the eyes not only of his countrymen but also of the British Government, and the day he set foot on India he received an invitation from Lord Willingdon, then Governor of Bombay, who as Viceroy of India became the Mahatma's adamant personal opponent in 1931.

"Gandhi," Willingdon said, "I want you to feel free to come to me any time you wish. Especially I want you to come to me whenever you decide to take action against the government." Was the Englishman shrewd enough to realize that Gandhi was a different man from the Indian politicians he had dealt with until then? In a land of talkers a man of action had arrived. In a country whose politics consisted of passing resolutions and drawing up petitions, a man had come who believed in taking "direct action." Was the Englishman aware that the tiny man with his winsome smile would become, in course of time, the greatest of "trouble-makers?" I believe he was, and that he would not otherwise have tried to elicit this promise from Gandhi.

It was always an affair filled with charm and courtesy when Gandhi met with an Englishman of the upper crust. Gandhi assured Lord Willingdon that he would indeed consult with him before taking any drastic action. "I do not have to give you a promise," he added. "It is always a custom with me to inform an adversary in advance about the measure I am going to employ against him. It is part of my creed of Truth."

The Englishman and the Indian found themselves equally eager to try the parliamentary procedure of negotiation before coming to any open break which obviously could only be resolved by recourse to direct action. Their reasonings were different. The Englishman was inspired by the traditions of law and precedence. All opposition to authority was welcome to him so long as it was fundamentally loyal and within the framework of law. To Gandhi, on the other hand, any fight was a necessary evil to be avoided until all peaceful procedures had failed.

As it turned out, their unwritten protocol was not to be tested for some time because Gandhi gave another promise to another man within a week. To my mind, the second promise was the soundest obligation that Gandhi ever undertook.

In those days, Gandhi was guided by a political mentor by the name of Gokhale. One of India's outstanding leaders, Gokhale had given long-distance help to Gandhi during the latter's South African struggles. When, within a week of his arrival, Gandhi reached Poona to pay his respects, Gokhale said to him, "Gandhi, I want you to promise me one thing, that for one solid year you will not participate in any political action, that you will silently tour the country to study the lay of the political land, and that you will not join a political party."

Thus began a strange year of fishing in political waters, attended by public silence, a year in which Gandhi laid the foundations of his movement and his organization in India.

There is a touch of the innkeeper in Gandhi's character. A motley crew always gathered around him wherever he stayed, wherever he went. For them he kept an open house, with Mrs. Gandhi as the busy hostess. From among them, he selected men and women of steel, people who would be the apostles of his teachings and the leaders of his various campaigns. Rounding them up, he had established, in 1910, a colony twenty-one miles from Johannesburg. Constant correspondent and "humble follower" of Tolstoy that he was, he had named his establishment the Tolstoy Farm. Now its inmates had come to India as he had, and there were several new candidates for admission. Gandhi was fully aware that much of his effectiveness in practical fields derived from associates who had dedicated their lives to his ideals.

Within three months of his arrival in India, on January 2, 1916, Gandhi found a place for them in Ahmedabad, the textile center of India. It was called Satyagraha Ashrama, after his movement, and those who joined it had to take several vows. They undertook always to be non-violent in thought, word and deed, to be truthful even though it might cost their lives, to control their palates, preferably taking, like Gandhi, not more than five articles of food in 24 hours, and never to eat after sundown. Courage and honesty were parts of their creed. One was bound, in addition, to speak in the vernacular and not in the alien English. Even husbands and wives were expected to live a celibate life. One was to use only articles produced in India—in order to stop the flow of national wealth from India to England. One wore only the homemade cloth known as Khaddar. One believed that the humbler one became the more one became noteworthy, just as the mango tree bows lower and lower the more fruit it bears. All were to live as one family, with a common kitchen. There was also a vow of non-possession, for an infinitesimal breach of which by his wife Gandhi once went on a three-day fast of atonement.

Although he refrained from politics, Gandhi could not be a bystander in the field of social reforms. To him, the greatest curse of India was the institution of untouchability, which regards the very touch of the outcasts among the Hindus as polluting. It is an extreme form of excommunication and social segregation. He shocked an orthodox audience by declaring: "I have felt that it is no part of real Hinduism to have in its hold a number of people whom I would call 'untouchables.' If it was proved to me that this is an essential part of Hinduism, I for one would declare myself an open rebel against Hinduism itself."

Laws and social revolution would indeed help in removing the evil, Gandhi felt, but these methods of change from outside would appeal more to the commissar type such as has been depicted by Arthur Koestler. What would appeal to the Yogi type, also described by Koestler, would and did appeal to Gandhi—namely, change from within. In the social struggles between those who believe that a group consists of nothing but individuals, and those who affirm that a group is more than the sum total of its members, Gandhi is on the side of the former. Moreover, leaders in the prophetic tradition have always considered personal example the ideal way of inspiring social change.

Shortly after organizing his new establishment, Gandhi invited Dudabhai and Daniben, an untouchable couple, to be members of his Ashrama. And Gandhi adopted as his own daughter (he is otherwise without a daughter, despite Bertrand Russell) their "mere toddling babe" called Lakshmi.

Equally prompt was the reaction of the Ahmedabad orthodoxy. The rich men stopped supporting Gandhi's new venture in community living, and the use of the public water well was forbidden to the inmates of his Ashrama. Gandhi, game but penniless, was about to move his colony to the untouchable quarters, when a money-lender drove up to his cottage, placed in his hands currency notes to the tune of 13,000 rupees, and sped away without even giving his name.

For, by then, Gandhi had been recognized as a Mahatma. Literally a Great Soul, the word Mahatma means a saint to the Hindus. In a letter dated February 18, 1915, Rabindranath Tagore, India's greatest poet since Kalidasa and a Nobel Prize winner, had written, "I hope that Mahatma and Mrs. Gandhi have arrived in Bolpur."

XIII. My Son, My Son

Natural forces within us are the true healers of disease.

—Hippocrates

Nearly all men die of their medicines, not of their diseases.

—Molière

A BOY was tossing in his bed, burning inside and mumbling in delirium. This ten-year-old had a severe attack of pneumonia combined with typhoid. Gandhi's second son, reaching a crisis of illness, had had no medical attendance, but was being treated by his father who had his own theories of healing.

More searing were the flames inside Gandhi's own mind. What was he to do? What would his wife think, and what would people say? That he let his son die on the altar of his experimentations? As he sat by the side of his son, Gandhi was fighting a battle on the field of his heart, torn between his convictions and the pressure of the deadly moment. Whenever he was about to give in, a contrary tide of thought would set in. Was he not giving his beloved son the very treatment he himself would take? What was more precious, the life of one's beloved or one's principles?

Earlier that day a doctor had warned Gandhi: "Your son is in grave danger. He will need the nourishment of eggs and chicken broth to carry him through the battle against death which he alone must fight."

Gandhi said that could not be. Hindu religious practice among the high caste forbade the nourishing of life through the murder of other lives. Life must indeed be saved, but there were severe limitations even in that vital pursuit. In this, Gandhi was at war with the cardinal Western medical principle, in application ever since the first magnificent statement of the Oath of Hippocrates, that the saving of life at all cost was the paramount duty of a doctor. Life is worth saving, beyond doubt, but not at all cost, argued Gandhi. There are principles for which men should be ready to die, accepting death willingly for their sake. And how was it that the life of a man was considered more worthy of preservation than that of a chicken? No, Gandhi the Hindu, with his beliefs in reincarnation, could not accept that, and he also felt that his son, had he the possession of his faculties, would have made the same choice. It was decided, therefore, that his son should do without eggs and broth and draw sustenance from diluted milk instead.

Opposed as he was to certain aspects of the practice of medicine, Gandhi dispensed with the doctor's advice and went ahead to employ hydropathic remedies. When his son had a moment of consciousness, Gandhi placed the problem before him, to hear in return, "Do try your hydropathic treatment, I will not have eggs or chicken." Heartened, Gandhi went on with his treatment.

He gave his son hip baths as prescribed by Kuhne the hydropathist. These lasted only three minutes each time; meanwhile, the boy got what nourishment he could from diluted orange juice.

His temperature remained high, often as much as 104 degrees. Lying beside his son, Gandhi found the child's body burning and parched. Not a single bead of perspiration was released. Gandhi got up, soaked a sheet in water, wrung the water out, and wrapped his son in it like an Egyptian mummy, exposing only the boy's head. Then, waking the mother to continue the vigil, he went outside to wander in the streets of Bombay.

The night was cool and a full moon was shining on the Chaupati Beach. Sweetmeat vendors were squatting on the soft white sand, holding umbrellas over their trays even though the drying sun had sunk beyond the waters hours ago; what was good protection against the sun was good against the moon. Around them, on low stools, sat their customers, eating the pungent sweets while ghee, or purified butter, dripped from their fingers. Nearby sat the Bhaiyas from Behar, whose special offering was small bubble breads made of wheat flour and served with chutney made of tamarind and ginger. The air was heavy with smells of saffron and coriander. A Moslem was selling pilao of partridges spiced with mace clove and pepper. A woman passed by with a basket of fruits balanced on her head and shouted that she had fresh juicy sappodillas and guava pears to sell. She displayed the bananas from the north, as dainty and tiny as lady's fingers, and as yellow as gold, while Gandhi walked past as if in a sleep. His eyes were turned inwards. She spat out on the curb the pink, pungent juice of betel leaf which colored her lips like rose petals, and stopped following the man who could be, she thought, only a poet or a madman. Gandhi rushed on, stumbling through the sidewalk flower-stalls laden with jasmine and roses and oleanders and lotuses. At a corner a couple was haggling, but Gandhi was unmindful of their whisperings as he was of the shouts of the barker enticing idlers to come in and see for themselves that a rope could rise from the ground, and that a man could climb it and vanish.

Gandhi was not indulging in an orgy of self-pity. Nor was he brooding, any more, on the question of the rightness or wrongness of the treatment he had been giving his son. He was simply praying, praying in the old Indian way. You repeat and repeat and repeat the name of God—in this case, Rama—and you clear your mind of all thoughts save that of the Lord's grace. It is called jap in India, and the locale Gandhi had selected for his prayers also was in the Yogi tradition. One need not be surrounded by the tranquil jungle or the isolated mountain cave. One can realize God's mercy in the midst of a madding and maddening crowd, provided one has the lotus-like quality of being in the water and yet untouched by it.

He did not know how long he had been walking. But

he returned home only when his legs were weary and when his tongue was heavy with naming the name of God.

"Is it you, Dad?" his son greeted him. Gandhi rushed to the bed, bent over, and saw that the boy's forehead was covered with beads of perspiration.

"Please pull me out. I can bear it no longer. I am perspiring all over and I feel as if I am in a burning oven," the boy pleaded.

Gandhi diverted his second son's mind with pleasantries, so that there would be enough time for the poison to drain out. Finally, he uncovered the child and dried his body, while the boy fell asleep in his arms.

The boy was on the mend and Gandhi felt that "God had saved my honor."

It is his religion of non-violence which makes Gandhi opposed to certain facets of the allopathic system of medicine, mostly perfected in the West. He is an opponent of vivisection, and he lacks Shaw's satire to suggest that medical researchers vivisect their mothers instead of animals. Always ready to dress wounds and to tend to the sick, Gandhi makes a faithful daily visit to the dispensary of his community. He organized an ambulance corps during the Boer War, and in England he seriously considered taking up medical studies; but, upon inquiry, he found that he would have to do vivisection, so he gave up the idea.

He is not opposed to medical research, however. "I have no objection to your dissecting dead bodies, and I have no objection to your holding post-mortem examinations. In fact, I think every dead body should be utilized in this manner, for the advance of medical science," he asserted. Here he clearly showed that he was not a religious bigot, for Hindu religion especially opposes any traffic with dead bodies of animals. But vivisection he abhors, and he declares that research will not really suffer in the long run. "In order to pump water to a higher level, you have to stop the lower outlets," Gandhi says. "Similarly, when you have eliminated certain methods of research, you will exercise your brains and ultimately find out some other humane means of doing the same thing." To carnivorous people, this squeamishness about animal life may seem far-fetched. But to Hindus it is definitely not.

It is not strictly India that speaks in Gandhi's nonviolence. It is Gandhi. He precipitated a minor crisis among the orthodox Jainas of Ahmedabad some years ago when he practiced mercy-killing of a calf in his hermitage who was suffering piteously and had no hope for recovery. Again, when monkeys, who are more numerous than men in Ahmedabad, began to pillage his crops, he sanctioned the use of stone-slings to frighten them away. If one of them had been killed . . . well, men must live! How many microbes we kill every time we breathe! Gandhi's non-violence is not esoteric; it is based on common sense.

Gandhi often prefers crude medicinal herbs, prepared the Ayurvedic way, to patent medicines for the simple reason that the masses of India are too poor to pay for the packaging which often costs more than the Western goods enclosed. He is strongly opposed to those practices which foster negligence and indulgence in the individual. "I overeat," he writes. "I have indigestion, I go to a doctor, he gives me medicine, I am cured, I overeat again, and I take his pills again. Had I not taken the pills in the first instance, I would have suffered the punishment deserved by me, and I would not have overeaten again. The doctor intervened and helped me to indulge myself. My body thereby certainly felt more at ease, but my mind became weakened." And mind-control, he asserts, is the main guide to physical health and spiritual progress. Gandhi has stated that his frequent high blood pressure is an indication of inadequate control over his mind. Certain practices of modern medicine are injurious to these basic principles, in his opinion. Instead of preparing an individual for a healthy and regulated life based on discipline born of experience, they prepare him to burn the candle of life at both ends. Preventive devices for venereal diseases and speedy control of social disease when it is contracted, instead of increasing the health rate of a community, deepen the moral degradation of its members.

Gandhi is supported by the latest Western trend when he refuses to separate mind from body in the treatment of human ailments. Man must be regarded as a whole. From this viewpoint, the next step is to become a follower of naturopathy. For the past fifty years, Gandhi has preferred hydrotherapy, earth treatment, fasting, and dietetics to other forms of cure better known in the West. If ailments are the result of a breach of nature's laws, they must be capable of cure by nature itself. If the process is a bit longer, it has its compensations. One learns to live more in tune with the laws of nature.

Gandhi, who has inspired so much spiritual fervor and faith among his countrymen, was incapable of founding his own religion. He is too much of an experimenter and a researcher—in the laboratory of the soul—to sanction any dogma, however personal. As a consequence, Gandhi himself has never been a Gandhi-ite, though millions have followed him blindly.

On January 12, 1924, Gandhi did a thing that many regard as an evidence of self-contradiction. Some followers thought that he sold "believers" down the river. But to those who know Gandhi's honor and chivalry, it was a supremely subtle example of "decency."

Gandhi was in jail, and he came down with an acute case of appendicitis. His life was in danger, and the English superintendent realized that the whole British Empire was on trial. Like an elephant, a dead Gandhi was more valuable than a live one to his followers any day. If Gandhi died in a British jail, there would be hell to pay. Stunned by the tragedy, the multitudes would avenge themselves on a government they would mistakenly hold responsible for Gandhi's death. The Englishman knew that only an operation could save the Mahatma. But he also knew about Gandhi's strange medical beliefs. Come what may, the Englishman decided to respect Gandhi's religion, and offered to let Gandhi try his own Ayurvedic treatment.

Gandhi was aware of the agonizing courage behind the Englishman's courtesy. He knew what was at stake. On the one hand, there was his own religious belief to be considered. On the other, there was the tremendous risk that his English keeper was taking, simply out of respect for Gandhi's faith. What would be said of him, and of the entire British Government, if he died in jail! How would his own followers interpret it! Not to be outdone in courtesy, Gandhi offered to abide by the best judgment of the Englishman, and put himself entirely in the latter's hands. "I am your prisoner," said Gandhi, "I cannot claim any privilege that cannot be claimed by other prisoners."

In the deep darkness of night, an English surgeon began the operation. There was no electricity in the jail, so an electric torch was used. When the operation was half-way through, it fused out, and the future of Indo-British relations hung in the balance. A nurse held a hurricane lantern in whose dim flickering light the operation was successfully completed. Gandhi has described the experience as "sacred," a credit to his jailors —the British—"and, I trust, to myself." In this world full of unpleasantness, if only men could fight it out with such grace!

XIV. The Warner

*If I shoved a plow, if I kept a flock, if I culti-
vated a garden, if I mended old clothes, no one
would notice me, few would consider me, not
many would find fault with me, and I could
easily please everybody. But for having been stu-
dious of the field of nature, solicitous for the
pasture of the soul, enamored of the cultivation
of the mind, a very Daedalus fashioning raiment
for the intellect, every passer-by threatens me,
every one who sees me attacks me, who comes
upon me rends me, who lays hold on me devours.
It is not one, it is not few; it is many, it is almost
all. If you would know why this is, I will tell you
the reason of it—I am a warner.*

—Edgar A. Singer

*Rise like lions after slumber
In unvanquishable number—
Shake your chains to earth, like dew
Which in sleep has fallen on you—
Ye are many, they are few.*

—Shelley

T HE sacred city of Benares
was the scene, the opening of the Benares Hindu
University the occasion, and February 4, 1916, the time.

On the banks of the holy Ganges, and under the shadow of Kashi Vishwanath temple, there had assembled a huge throng, but it was more like a galaxy of stars. There were pundits and there were world-famous professors. And there were political leaders and government officials, wealthy Zamindars and merchant princes, all vying with each other in ostentation. The Viceroy had come and gone, and today's star speaker was Gandhi, who had recently returned from South Africa and who had just finished a year of self-imposed political apprenticeship which had been eloquent with public silence. This was to be his first political speech in India, his first plunge into Hindustani turmoil. People were curious. What strange things would the stranger have to say, they asked themselves.

"It is a matter of deep humiliation and shame for us," Gandhi declared, "that I am compelled this evening under the shadow of this great college, in this sacred city, to address my countrymen in a language that is foreign to me." What was he saying, his listeners asked each other. How did he dare! How very audacious of the newcomer! Wasn't he aware that all educated Indians spoke in English, and that it was a matter of distinction to be able to speak the tongue of the Viceroy? Or was he simply trying to shock them to get attention, newcomer that he was?

But Gandhi had not even made his point. He added: "The charge against us is that we have no initiative. How can we have any if we devote precious years of our life to the mastery of a foreign tongue?" Then he let go with his Parthian shot, "We fail in this attempt also."

Almost the first sentence of his first political address on the soil of India thus landed like a bombshell. The West, represented by such eminent persons as Annie Besant, was laughing in its sleeve at the spectacle of English being denounced in English. The East, subtly snobbish about aping the Englishman, felt chilly under this indecent exposure.

Gandhi gazed in another direction and continued, "His Highness the Maharajah who presided yesterday over our deliberations spoke about the poverty of India. . . . But what did we witness in the great pandal in which the foundation ceremony was performed by the Viceroy? Certainly a most gorgeous show, an exhibition of jewelry which made a splendid feast for the eyes of the greatest jeweler who chose to come from Paris. I compare with the richly bedecked noblemen the millions of the poor. And I feel like saying to these noblemen, 'There is no salvation for India unless you strip yourselves of this jewelry and hold it in trust for your countrymen in India.'"

There was an uneasy stir in the audience. Hadn't the man any tact, they wondered! Was he such a fool he had not noticed all the Maharajahs and noblemen on the dais? Any one of them could order his henchmen to assassinate the Bania on the spot and could escape the consequences. But Gandhi wasn't through. He fixed his eyes upon the "bedecked noblemen" and said casually, "I am sure it is not the desire of the King-Emperor or Lord Hardinge that in order to show the truest loyalty

to our King-Emperor, it is necessary for us to ransack
our jewelry-boxes and to appear bedecked from top to
toe. I would undertake, at the peril of my life, to bring
to you a message from King George himself that he ex-
pects nothing of the kind."

A faint laughter was breaking at the edges of the
throng where sat the less fortunate and, consequently,
the less bedecked. The newcomer's humor began to win
him applause.

It was apparent by then that Gandhi was out for
blood, and he promptly tossed a third bomb at the
gathering by "openly discussing" the cult of the Bengal
Bomb Throwers who were variously known as the
"terrorists" and "anarchists." It became too much for
Mrs. Besant, whose concept of revolution was well-
rounded by Fabian legalism; she realized that even listening to what Gandhi was now saying could be inter-
preted as treason and she cried, "Please stop it." Gandhi
turned to the chairman, who was given only a Hobson's
choice. The audience was warming up. They wanted
more of Gandhi. A green light was forced.

The man was preposterous! He went on to tell
Maharajahs they should clean the streets, to ask the
priests to clean the temples of Benares, and to urge the
high castes not to ill-treat the low castes in railway compartments. For "No amount of speeches will ever make
us fit for self-government. It is only our conduct that
will fit us for it."

Then came the climax, and since this was 1916, and a
war-year, it was a dangerous utterance, to say the least.

The Warner

Said Gandhi: "If I found it necessary for the salvation of India that the English should retire, that they should be driven out, I would not hesitate to declare that they would have to go, and I hope I would be prepared to die in defence of that belief."

But the time was not yet. Only two months before the Viceroy, Lord Hardinge, had conferred upon Gandhi the Kaiser-i-Hind Gold Medal for his loyal services to the Empire in South Africa. Not that Gandhi was unaware of the defects in British rule, but he thought that "It was on the whole acceptable. In those days I believed that the British rule was on the whole beneficial to the ruled." So much so that he once recalled that "Hardly ever have I known anybody to cherish such loyalty as I did to the British Constitution."

As a schoolboy, like all other schoolboys in government institutions, he had often sung the British national anthem and enjoyed it. Later, in South Africa, he had joined in the singing with other loyal sons and daughters of the Empire. As he grew in spiritual consciousness, however, he became a bit disturbed about the contents of "God Save the King." But his criticism was aesthetic and ethical, not political. The lines

> Scatter her enemies,
> And make them fall;
> Confound their politics,
> Frustrate their knavish tricks

jarred upon his sensitivities. How arrogant of anyone to assume that his so-called enemies must be knaves,

Gandhi argued with himself. And how can people become automatically wrong simply because they are enemies? "From God we could only ask for justice," he wrote. To tell God that a side is right because it is our side and to commit Him to such prejudiced protection sounded a bit naïve and illogical. Still, he was proud to sing the anthem because at that time his own opposition, if any, was His Majesty's Loyal Opposition.

During the Christmas of that year, at the Congress session in Lucknow, loyal Gandhi noticed a young man with fire in his eyes, a young man who was out to put an *r* in front of the Mahatma's evolution. He was Jawaharlal Nehru, son of Gandhi's friend Motilal. But the man who was later to be announced as Gandhi's successor found the Mahatma, at their first meeting, "very distant and different and unpolitical."

XV. Empire on Trial

> *When any people are ruled by laws in framing which they have no part, that are to bind them to all intents and purposes, without, in the same manner, binding the legislators themselves, they are, in the strictest sense, slaves; and the government, with respect to them, is despotic.*
>
> —Alexander Hamilton

> *Laws, like cobwebs, entangle the weak, but are broken by the strong.*
>
> —Solon

THE scene shifts from sacred Benares to smoky Ahmedabad. In place of the myriad domes of the Holy City are found the hundred chimneys of a hundred textile mills which cover the city with soot and give it a Pittsburgh-like look. On either side of the River Sabramati are to be seen the monuments of the old Mohammedan rule, craning their necks, as it were, over the foliage of tamarind trees. Although not sacred, the monkeys enjoy the freedom of the city simply because they are too numerous to cage.

It was a Saturday noon, March 18, 1922. The populace was tense with suppressed excitement. The whole nation was hushed. For the Great Trial had begun, and no trial before it had been packed with so much drama since the day when jesting Pilate asked, "What is truth?"

In the small Circuit Court at Shahi Bag sat Gandhi, facing District and Sessions Judge C. N. Broomsfield, charged with "bringing or attempting to bring into hatred or contempt or exciting or attempting to excite disaffection towards His Majesty's Government, established by law in British India." Section 124-A of the Indian Penal Code, which had sent several illustrious patriots to jail before, had been invoked.

An English Advocate-General was conducting the prosecution. The accused was undefended.

Gandhi pleaded guilty to all the charges, but the Advocate-General was not satisfied. He went on to recite the whole life-history of Gandhi to prove that it was nothing but the career of a rebel.

As Gandhi sat there, tolerantly smiling at the unnecessary rigmarole, he must have mulled over in his mind—since he later set them forth in his formal statement—all the steps that led up to his present state. It was the evolution of "a staunch loyalist and co-operator" into "an uncompromising disaffectionist and Non-co-operator." It was the story of a defender of the British Empire who developed "almost a passion" to preach disaffection toward the existing system of government.

As Gandhi listened with one ear to a version of his

life made harrowing and hair-raising by the English
Advocate-General, he was aware of the supreme ironical
twist taken by his loyalism. Time was when he gave the
government his "voluntary and hearty co-operation,
criticising it freely where I felt it was faulty but never
wishing its destruction." He mentally recalled his services to the Empire, rendered with a sense of duty and
never in hope of reward. . . .

When the Boers challenged and threatened the Empire in 1899, Gandhi offered his services to the Crown,
raised a volunteer ambulance corps, and tended to the
front trenches during the relief of Ladysmith.

Again, to aid the Empire during the Zulu "rebellion"
of 1906, Gandhi raised a stretcher-bearer party. On both
these occasions he was awarded medals and mentioned
in despatches.

He was in London when the war broke out between
England and Germany in 1914. He promptly raised another volunteer ambulance corps from among the Indian
students attending English universities.

Back in India, he had been invited by Lord Chelms-
ford to Delhi in 1918 to attend the War Conference. It
was the darkest hour of the Empire at war. Over the
protest of his colleagues, he went out recruiting Indians
as soldiers, and broke his health; for he believed that "it
was possible by such services to gain a status of full
equality in the Empire."

. . . As he thought of his former devotion, so Gandhi
thought of the events that convinced him that the only
honorable course open to him was revolt. . . .

The first shock had come in 1919. India had expected to be granted a status similar to that of a Dominion as a reward for her war services. She had contributed more men than all the Dominions put together. Gandhi was in no small way responsible for the expectations of India at this time. But India was not rewarded. Instead she was handed the Rowlatt Act which deprived her of whatever little freedom of speech and press and assembly she had enjoyed before. For some time Gandhi was mentally paralyzed by the disillusionment. Slowly recovering from a feeling of impotence and helplessness, he hit upon an idea. As he later told C. R. Rajagopalachari, "The idea came to me last night in a dream, that we should call upon the country to observe a general hartal," or a cessation of all business, even more complete than a general strike, but observed in a spirit of mourning.

Episode followed episode. The government matched its brawn against the people's non-violent protests—in Bombay, in Madras, in Calcutta. After a short tour of South India, Gandhi was back in Bombay where he heard that the police had opened fire on a peaceful procession in Delhi on March 30.

Meanwhile he had received an urgent summons for help from the Punjab where the government had struck with fury and might, and where there had developed a dangerously explosive situation. Facing the English judge and half-listening to the English Advocate-General, the Mahatma's memory must have flashed back to the happenings which culminated in the Massacre of

Amritsar, a turning point in the thinking and life not only of Gandhi but of most Indians.

Gandhi still was clinging to his belief that the English could be touched by reason and by an appeal to their sense of fair play. Englishmen were still thinking that, although he made them uncomfortable, Gandhi was no outlaw or rebel.

At the time of the massacre, Amritsar was humming with Baishakhi festival pilgrims, who had come to catch a glimpse of the Golden Temple. Religious fervor was tinged with political fever brought on by the Rowlatt Act. On top of it all, the government spirited away leaders of the Punjab on the night of April 10.

On April 13, a meeting was held in Jallianwala Bag. Although General Dyer, a British Army officer, had the night before issued an order prohibiting public meetings, the public was not aware of it. Some twenty thousand unsuspecting men, women, and children gathered together in the Bag, a walled-in garden with a single entrance which was also the only exit. All were peaceful and pledged to Gandhian non-violence, and unarmed. Suddenly General Dyer arrived on the scene with fifty soldiers armed with machine-guns. He posted his troops at the exit and, without warning, gave order to fire. Some 1,650 rounds were fired in ten minutes. When Dyer withdrew, some (according to the *Non-Official Inquiry Committee's Report*) 1,200 dead and 3,600 wounded were lying in the garden. According to the official *Hunter Commission Report*, about 400 were killed and between 1,000 and 2,000 wounded. The nation was stunned.

It is important that English testimony be cited here, even at the risk of repetition, since Amritsar remains a sore point of contention on either side. Writes Edward Thompson: "In April, 1919, General Dyer shot down nearly two thousand people in the death-trap of that sunken garden at Jallianwala, in Amritsar, where the wounded were left all night to crawl and cry out. There followed the provocation of infamous debates in both British Houses of Parliament, and of the mean agitation that whipped up a subscription of £26,000 to the Dyer Testimonial Fund."

That was not all. There was a street in Amritsar which no Indian could pass except crawling on his belly. There were public floggings.

A curious incident took place while Gandhi was serving on the Non-Official Committee which investigated the Massacre of Amritsar for three months and examined nearly two thousand witnesses. M. R. Jayakar, who was also on the committee, tells that detailed and circumstantial evidence, which could have been eagerly believed in the agony of the tragedy, was pressed upon the investigators, making out that General Dyer had "deliberately lured" the people into the walled-in garden, in order to make an easy slaughter of them. Gandhi was pressed from all sides by the furious and the humiliated. But the Mahatma brushed them all aside, ignoring the outraged insistence of his own people. "I do not believe it," he said, "and it shall not be set down in the Report."

. . . He reasoned with himself, as he faced the English

judge, that along with him the whole Empire was on trial. At last, he was standing, reading his prepared statement. "If one has no affection for a person or a system," he said, "one should be free to give the fullest expression to his disaffection, so long as he does not contemplate, promote or incite to violence." And nobody could deny that Gandhi had always been true to his professions of non-violence.

Looking at the judge and far beyond him, Gandhi announced in a gentle but firm voice, "I hold it to be a virtue to be disaffected towards a Government which in its totality has done more harm to India than any previous system. India is less manly under the British rule than she ever was before." He was thus invoking the final right to revolution which the American constitution grants to an aggrieved and outraged people. He was invoking something higher.

"I am here, therefore," he continued evenly, "to invite and submit cheerfully to the highest penalty that can be inflicted upon me for what in law is a deliberate crime and what appears to me to be the highest duty of a citizen." Here was posed a conflict between man-made law, which can be an instrument for the perpetuation of people in power, and the law of the free conscience, which is at the foundation of all systems of ethics. It was not a call to anarchy, but to a higher order. Again it was a conflict between the vertical and horizontal trends in man. Should man prostrate himself in order to conform to man-made rules, or should he stand erect in the light of God? Gandhi's was a challenge and not a plea for mercy. He knew that he had played with fire and aroused the wrath of powers that be. But he was so sure of his stand that he let it be known that were he to be set free, he would still do the same.

Then Gandhi posed the supreme conflict between English law and the eternal verities, the conflict of Reinhold Niebuhr's moral man and immoral society, of Yogi principles and British protocol, of historic man and his eternal destiny. "The only course open to you, the Judge," he faced the magistrate with humility, "is either to resign your post and thus dissociate yourself from evil, if you feel that the law you are called upon to administer is an evil and that in reality I am innocent; or to inflict on me the severest penalty if you believe that the system and the law you are assisting to administer are good for the people of this country and that my activity is therefore injurious to the public weal."

With that he sat down. Did he expect a conversion on the part of the judge, as had happened in cases of many Indian magistrates trying Gandhi's Satyagrahis? He had said at the outset, however, that he did not expect that kind of conversion, but he did expect to make his meaning clear by the time he had finished his statement. So Gandhi was actually expecting the pronouncement of sentence.

The Englishman, who was conscious that he himself was also on trial, was equal to the occasion from any mortal standard, if not in the light of the timeless truth to which saints subscribe. Judge Broomsfield said: "The law is no respecter of persons. Nevertheless, it will be impossible to ignore the fact that you are in a different category from any person I have ever tried or am likely to have to try. It would be impossible to ignore the fact that, in the eyes of millions of your countrymen, you are a great patriot and a great leader. Even those who differ from you in politics look upon you as a man of high ideals and of noble and of even saintly life."

Declining to judge Gandhi on that ground, the Englishman said something which is amazingly typical of the Western mind. He considered it his duty to judge the Mahatma only "as a man subject to law." The Western habit is to establish, first, a frame of reference, second, to fit man's conduct neatly into it, so that everything becomes legal—and therefore all right. This pattern of thinking is a source of worldly strength, because only delimited categories can produce zeal. Universal men with cosmic patterns of thought are likely to be abstract, "unrealistic," and thus incapable of immediate effectiveness.

Judge Broomsfield went on: "There are probably few people in India who do not sincerely regret that you should have made it impossible for any government to leave you at liberty. But it is so." In that sincere and tremulous admission of a fair and legalistic Englishman is packed the schizophrenia of the modern age. We glimpse the truth but dare not follow it. We feel so naked under the cosmic rays of eternal truth that we prefer to read by earthen lamps. We tremble to stand in the presence of prophets, so we worship them after they are dead. Bernard Shaw's observation in the epilogue of *Saint Joan,* that each age must crucify its prophet, is also a warning. For the modern age cannot afford the things that past ages could afford. The weapons of past ages, howsoever diabolical, were nevertheless nondestructive of matter in the scientific sense of the term. In the eyes of nuclear physicists, whenever we destroyed one physical form, we unknowingly created another, because we were using only the surface of atoms. But now we have learned to explode and release the basic energy of the universe, and this release of energy is achieved only by the *disintegration* of matter. In former, and even quite recent, ages our material world in its totality was always safe. But now that we know how to cause disintegration of matter itself, creation itself is threatened.

Conforming to the accepted but limited mores of the modern age, Broomsfield sentenced Gandhi to six years' simple imprisonment, but added with typical British charm and probity, "If the course of events in India should make it possible for the Government to reduce the period and release you, no one will be better pleased than I."

Gandhi responded to English amiability with Oriental gallantry, saying, "So far as the sentence is concerned, I certainly consider that it is as light as any judge would inflict on me, and so far as the whole proceedings are concerned, I must say that I could not have expected greater courtesy." The Judge left the court and the Mahatma's followers fell at his feet.

XVI. An Artist of Life

It is a gratification to me to know that I am ignorant of art.

—Mark Twain

I know I have earned notoriety as a philistine in art.

—Gandhi

Some years passed, and Gandhi came back to his hermitage. One evening, as usual, the spiritual orgy of prayer at the ashrama was being quickened by two persons—Gandhi and Pandit Khare. The latter was the ashrama musician, selected by Gandhi from among the greatest practitioners of Hindustani music because Pandit Khare had a devotional bent of mind.

Gandhi was still to deliver his sermon. But Pandit Khare was leading the group in an exalting recitation of one of Mira's songs begging the Lord to hire her as His maid. While the Pandit continued, a boy emerged from behind the bushes and whispered something in Gandhi's ears. Everything went on as usual.

When the singing was over, Gandhi calmly announced that he had just been told that Pandit Khare's son had died. He looked at the musician.

"May I sing one more song, Bapu?" asked the ashrama singer, whose son had passed away a few minutes before in a hut hardly thirty yards away.

"Yes, you may, as a prayer for the dearly departed," Gandhi said.

The devotee-singer began to sing his favorite song, and presently lost himself in its uplifting elation. But Gandhi sat there, calmly going over the developments of the past few days of which the infant's death was a climax.

An epidemic of smallpox had crossed the river and gripped Gandhi's ashrama. Some physicians of Ahmedabad had come forward ready to vaccinate the youngsters of Gandhi's establishment. But the Mahatma had thankfully declined their services on the ground that the use of cowpox was contrary to the Hindu religion and to his own doctrine of non-violence. But this he had done only after receiving the unanimous consent of his group. Contending that it is good for the future health of the child to have the dormant poison ousted from his body through smallpox, Gandhi had been administering his earth-treatment to the sick. There had been, however, several deaths, and now the infant son of his favorite musician was no more. It was at his behest, and mainly through his personal inspiration, that the ashramites had refused to allow the administration of vaccination. Was he not, therefore, responsible for the demise of several children?—he must have asked himself as he sat there silently without betraying a trace of emotion.

When the time came to speak, Gandhi again exhorted his followers to resort to vaccination if they were afraid to follow his lonely path. But all agreed to abide by his teachings. Silently they rose, with heavy hearts, and watched Gandhi put his arm around the bereaved musician, walking away toward the cottage where the boy lay dead.

Gandhi thus used music to console the man who had lost his son, and for the edification of the departed soul. It was typical of his attitude toward art. He used art as the church uses it—as a spiritual prop.

Artistic experience to him is an auxiliary to moral striving. It puts man more in tune with eternity and with lasting values of life. It refines one's senses so that they are more ready to appreciate experience which is not of the body. It reigns supreme in the field of spiritual propaganda. Gandhi also believed in harnessing art for propaganda and education in a just cause. But it seems that art to Gandhi was something to be used and not to be enjoyed, something ennobling, not simply joy-giving. Most thinkers have indeed discarded the idea of art for art's sake, and yet they grant that aesthetic experience can be as self-sufficient and fundamental as spiritual or religious experience. Without saying so, Gandhi seems to have denied this. Aesthetic experience was not quite fundamental to him nor so self-sufficient. It was an aid, a powerful support, perhaps, to religious experience.

As pointed out above, this is the church view of art. In India, all traditional art forms have been religious, invoked in the name of religious utility, so much so that most ancient paintings were of gods and nymphs rather than of men and women. Poets did describe feminine contours in voluptuous vocabularies, and the ecstasy of union, but always they depicted the acts of gods and goddesses. And temples were the greatest patrons of artists. Modern Western ideas were about to set Indian art free from religious confines when Gandhi unintentionally inspired a revival of the old forms.

Many Gujarati writers are at variance with this view. They consider Gandhi to be a great writer and point to his crystal-clear and unadorned, almost primitive prose style. But there is in this tendency a trace of that English idolatry which contends that Shakespeare was a sound physician. Even such a great painter as Nanda Lal Bose describes the Mahatma as "the true artist," and cites as evidence Gandhi's eye for minute but not inconsequential detail, the neatness of everything he does and surrounds himself with, and his insistence on the utter sincerity of artistic expression. "I do not want an expert pianist," Gandhi wrote, "but a sincere and devoted fiddler." Also to Gandhi's credit is his primitivistic theory of a crafstmen's society, wherein each product would bear the distinctive imprint of the individual craftsman who made it through creative delight. These are important artistic values, but they do not in themselves constitute art.

The fact that Gandhi is an artist of life, making deft

use of accepted art forms, sometimes fools enthusiasts into believing that he is a great writer or a great art expert. He has devoted his whole life to developing his own personality, has believed in being himself, and has made heroes out of men of clay, thus mastering the greatest art of all, the art of living. But that does not make him an artist as the term is usually employed.

Yet he has inspired poetry and drama, painting and music, as no other man in India's recent history. The ferment he has created in the political and social field has filtered into various art forms, given new zest to creative minds, provided them with the secular religion of social consciousness, and brought about almost a renaissance in the art world of India. For life, like a fine stringed instrument, vibrates throughout when touched sensitively on a major chord.

Because Gandhi blasted the inhibitions of Indian artists by giving them a sense of cultural pride, he is sometimes mistaken as the leader of artistic endeavor. In grateful creative minds, the fact is ignored that those who express themselves through the fine arts do not quite measure up in Gandhi's estimation. So far as the ascetic Mahatma is concerned, the creator is not quite so heroic as the doer. To him, a religious leader, or a social reformer, or a statesman, or even a laborer is more in the heroic tradition than is a creative mind. Gandhi is slightly more suspicious of artists than was Lenin of the intellectuals.

The modern poet's hero will share with Gandhi's hero the qualities of solitariness and of prophetic insight.

But whereas the composite modern poet would be filled with the idea of personal unhappiness, Gandhi would prefer a man whose experience of unhappiness is vicarious, who has, that is, a consciousness of collective unhappiness around him. And in place of the poet's aesthetic intensity, Gandhi would choose religious intensity. But what Gandhi would most condemn in the modern poet is his personal maladjustment to the world, wherein he lives in the protective shell of his own mind, evolving his own private symbolism and a language which progressively loses touch with the idioms of common understanding. Gandhi likes Wordsworth's "Lucy Grey" because it can be understood by adolescents as well as by adults. Gandhi prefers Tulsidas's *Ramayana* to Valmiki's because it is simpler; in this, he ignores the psychological fact that intelligence can be measured in proportion to the ability to make distinctions. What is Gandhi to make of the modern poet, so hard to follow, who is so surprised when you understand him that he confronts you with the cold stare of a man who has been intruded upon.

The well-buttressed melancholy and the nagging disbelief of the modern artist are in sharp contrast to what Gandhi thinks would electrify the masses—buoyant enthusiasm, vital energy, and ebullient optimism. Gandhi himself is in revolt against modern machines that are obliterating human values, but his is a hopeful and collective and constructive revolution, while the modern poet's is an individual revolt against society, which makes him a somber symbolist with a raven perched over his door. Gandhi would prefer a deed to a poem or a painting any day. The notion that individual refinement through art will result in the refinement of collective action—well, Gandhi has no time for such speculation, just as Buddha had no time for God.

XVII. A Fool of God

*Can you walk on water? You have done no
better than a straw. Can you fly in the air? You
have done no better than a bluebottle. Conquer
your heart; then you may become somebody.*

— Ansari of Herat

*In 1769 a Harvard disputation decided in the
affirmative the question whether reptiles in
America originated with those preserved by
Noah.*

— Merle Curti

At THIS point, we turn
from the artistic to the miraculous. In the "Gandhian
war" year of 1930, I witnessed an incident which convinced me that, although he was often mystic in his approach, the Mahatma was not mediumistic by intent.

One morning a group of villagers approached our
camp in Karadi, a small hamlet in Gujarat. They were
marching in a procession, women singing religious songs
and forming the vanguard. The men behind were bearing fruits and flowers and bags of money.

They circled around our temporary dwellings, then

[126]

proceeded toward Gandhi's hut, made of mud walls and grass roof, umbrellaed by the foliage of a mango tree. The menfolk came forward and placed their offerings, as if at the feet of an image of Buddha.

Gandhi was spinning cotton yarn. He was visibly puzzled by the spectacle. He beckoned the headman and gently inquired what was meant by this display.

The headman faltered. Then he told a strange story. It seemed that the village had a well, but the well had yielded no water for years and years; the women had to go to a nearby village each day to fetch drinking water in earthen pitchers which they gracefully balanced on their heads. But the day Gandhi's feet touched the soil of the village, the water came rising up from the bottom of the well which had been barren. (The story turned out to be true on later investigation.)

"We have come to worship you," the headman said, "for you must be an incarnation of Rama, the Great God."

There was no smile on Gandhi's face now. He had turned stern, like a father who finds that his children have gone too far. "That is foolish and unbecoming of you," he told the group. "I have no more influence with God than you have."

And then he became kind again, and began to explain away the mystery in terms of rural allegory. "Suppose what you say has happened. Surely it was a coincidence." He paused for a while, mending a broken thread. "Now take the instance of a crow who sits on a palm tree just at the moment the tree falls to the ground. Do you think that it was the weight of the crow which caused the tree's uprooting?"

Then Gandhi commanded them to go back to their homes, and admonished them not to waste time in speculating about his divinity but to use their time and energy to free Mother India.

When a man, during his lifetime, is looked up to by millions as a prophet—and that is the case with Gandhi— he is a great man. But when such a man has the humility to deny godhead, he is greater still. In spite of unprecedented lures that have been put before him during his lifetime, Gandhi remains a man among men, instead of assuming the role of the fountainhead of a new religion.

Indians are especially quick to accept outstanding leaders like Gandhi as incarnations of God. The tradition is handed down from *The Bhagavad Gita*, wherein the Lord hath spoken:

> . . . *When Righteousness*
> *Declines, O Bharat!, when Wickedness*
> *Is strong, from age to age, I rise, and take*
> *Visible shape, and move a man with man,*
> *Succoring the good, thrusting the evil back,*
> *And setting Virtue on her throne again.*

According to *Puranas*, there have already been nine such avataras, or incarnations of God. The imminent one is to be Kalki.

Around 1920 a story was bandied about which supported this myth. Gandhi was being driven in an automobile from one village to another in the Province of

Behar. An old blind woman had heard that he was to pass by her hamlet, but that he was not scheduled to stop there. She trudged through the furrowed fields and sat by the dirt road waiting to hear the sound of the Mahatma's automobile. When Gandhi's car reached the spot where the woman sat, a tire went flat. As the occupants got out to await the repairs, Gandhi's eyes fell on the blind woman whom he approached with the respect due to the aged and to the blind, who in India are called "divine-eyed." The old creature perceived the hand of God in the accident.

The stories of miraculous healings and of Gandhi's disappearances from jail in order to tend to the ailing are endless. Gandhi is aware of all this, and as a result he has never tired of denying his divinity, and lest a cult of succession should start, Gandhi has never pushed his sons forward. His friends have noticed, on the contrary, a tendency on his part to bury his sons in useful but unspectacular social service.

XVIII. *Pilgrims to the Sea*

Not as the conqueror comes,
They, the true-hearted came;
Not with the roll of the stirring drums,
And the trumpet that sings of fame.
—Felicia Hemans

IT WAS an eventful night a year after the water-well episode. The Indian moon, which inexplicably looks brighter than the same moon shining in colder climes, made the marble palaces of New Delhi stand out stark in the solitude of midnight. Here was the British-created city, a replica of Washington, on the very outskirts of the fabled ruins of vanished older empires. Here was an amazing architecture, a garish blend of Buddhist gargoyles and Hellenist pillars, whose outlines seemed even more anachronistic in the moonlight.

The most conspicuous palace, called, with the British knack for understatement, the Viceregal Lodge, symbol of all the pomp and circumstance of the Empire, was burning midnight lamps on this night of March 4, 1931. It was entertaining a most incongruous guest amidst all the splendor and ceremony, and at an unusual hour, when most Indians are in bed.

The Viceroy, who was then Lord Irwin and who later became Viscount Halifax, was in conference with Mahatma Gandhi. It was quite un-English behavior, to say the least. It was so much out of British character that Winston Churchill, in a fit of protocolics, shouted angrily in the House of Commons about "the half-naked fakir [who] strode up the steps of the Viceroy's palace."

The circumstances in which the meeting took place were even more outrageous to Churchillian Tories, to whom even the idea of Dominion status for India was a "crime" and who could not visualize, "in any foreseeable future," India as an equal partner in the Commonwealth. For, on this particular night a cornered Empire was negotiating with an erstwhile rebel and concluding what came to be known as the Gandhi-Irwin Pact.

As the towering Englishman and tiny Indian faced each other across the table—the Crown's representative and the "Uncrowned King of India"—ready to place their respective signatures on the document, they must have reviewed in their minds the months of stormy struggle, involving hundreds of deaths and thousands of imprisonments and resulting in a complete paralysis of the British administration. But compared to the memory of the Viceroy, who had arrived in India only four years before, the Mahatma's was longer. . . .

After his premature release from prison on account of poor health, and at the conclusion of several regional struggles which he had led, Gandhi had consented to be-

come the president of the Indian National Congress
which met in Belgaum during the Christmas vacation of
1924. Gandhi always preferred the role of president-
maker to that of president, and this was the first and last
year of the Mahatma's formal presidency of the mammoth political party.

An advocate of more action and fewer words, Gandhi's
address was noted as the shortest on record. It was no
mean achievement in long-winded India. But the session
was more memorable for another of Gandhi's actions.
Gandhi felt that the young man with a dream in his eye,
whom he had first observed in 1916 and always kept in
mind, was now ready for a greater opportunity. He persuaded the party to appoint Jawaharlal Nehru the general secretary of the Indian National Congress.

There developed a father-and-son affection between
the two, and there followed years of close collaboration.
But the younger and more impatient man was slowly
coming to the conclusion that India's inevitable destiny
was complete sovereignty and absolute severance of
British ties, while Gandhi was still clinging to the idea
of Dominion status within the Commonwealth. At the
1926 Congress session Nehru openly advocated his
creed, but the resolution failed because of Gandhi's opposition. The younger man again moved the Independence Resolution at the Congress meeting the following
year, and, in Gandhi's absence, it passed. Commented
Gandhi in his weekly *Young India:* "The Congress stul-
tifies itself by repeating year after year resolutions of
this character when it knows that it is not capable of

carrying them into effect." His was a protest not against the ideal but against youthful bravado. The younger man was pinning his faith on the inspiring quality of magic words.

The question again came up during the Calcutta session of the Congress in 1928. The situation was more personal than ever and a triangular one. Against Jawaharlal Nehru were arrayed Gandhi as well as his own father Motilal, who was presiding over the annual meeting. The older men pleaded for patience and for Dominion status. But the younger man carried the day. It was resolved that the Congress should advocate independence for India if Dominion status were not forthcoming by the end of 1929.

At the stroke of midnight, December 31, 1929, Gandhi moved the resolution, proclaiming independence to be the goal of India. Jawaharlal Nehru, who had valiantly battled for years for this new political outlook, was presiding over that fateful Lahore session of the Congress.

Retiring to his hermitage for heart-searching, and drawing his inspiration from the American Declaration of Independence, Gandhi drafted the pledge, whose opening paragraph was: "We believe that it is the inalienable right of the Indian people, as of any other people, to have freedom and to enjoy the fruits of their toil and have the necessities of life so that they may have full opportunities of growth. We believe also that if any government deprives a people of these rights and oppresses them, the people have a further right to alter it or to abolish it. The British government in India has not only deprived the Indian people of their freedom but has based itself on the exploitation of the masses, and has ruined India economically, politically, culturally and spiritually. We believe, therefore, that India must sever the British connection and attain Purna Swaraj or complete independence." On January 26, 1930, people all over the country took the independence pledge.

Making sure that "the fire and the fervor are there in the people," Gandhi decided to lead the entire nation in a campaign of civil disobedience and Satyagraha to end the British rule. But the chivalry of his non-violence would not permit him the advantages of a surprise attack. So he chose a young English disciple of his to convey his ultimatum to the Viceroy on March 22, 1930. It contained a last-minute plea for the satisfaction of India's demands, and outlined all the steps that Gandhi contemplated taking in case of rejection. He addressed Lord Irwin as "Dear Friend," and went on to say, "Before embarking on civil disobedience and taking the risk I have dreaded to take all these years, I would fain approach you and find a way out." To the Englishman it was again a question of law and not of "inalienable rights" or "self-evident truths." The beauty of democracy is that it tolerates opposition. But even democracy cannot afford to tolerate any opposition other than "loyal." That should suffice in a democracy because it provides that the people always have a chance to vote down an oppressive regime. But had India any such opportunity of making its will clear at the polls and making election results effective? Even sincere Englishmen have acted confused in India; for sincere as they are, they have been aware that their presence in India itself is confusing. Irwin only regretted "to hear that Mr. Gandhi intended to contravene the law."

Gandhi announced: "On bended knees I asked for bread and received a stone instead." He called upon the people to engage themselves in a "war of independence."

On the morning of March 12, the historic March to the Sea started. Gandhi was leading the small group in what looked like a pilgrimage, but around his band marched thousands of villagers who were replaced by fresh thousands at each stop. The march fired the imagination of the people because it reminded them of the wanderings of the Buddha to free the minds of men. As we marched, people came to us with flowers and coconuts, bedecking us as if we were horses of sacrifice. We youngsters had to run in order to keep pace with our leader, whose stride was measured by the reveille that thundered in his soul. And wherever we stopped, the villagers put us up, brought food, and provided shelter. When on April 6, after a two-hundred mile march, we reached Port Dandi, the nation was awaiting, with bated breath, the signal from the Mahatma which would send it on a path of lawbreaking aimed at paralyzing British rule. At first, only the government monopoly over salt manufacture was to be attacked, through the making of contraband salt, because all Indians, especially the poor, were affected by that law. But the ultimate goal was to break all the laws of an unjust order and thus to refuse to recognize it.

Monster meetings took place in cities, while villages organized bands of civil resisters who broke the law en masse. Police arrested Nehru, and opened fire in Peshawar, Solapur, Karachi, Ratnagiri, Patna. . . .

The Northwest Frontier was active under the leadership of Abdul Ghaffar Khan, the Frontier Gandhi. Moslem women shed their veils and came out in the open. A British officer ordered his men to fire, but the Garhwali soldiers refused. They were court-martialed.

I was rudely awakened by the pounding of military boots at 12:45 A.M. one morning. In no time the whole camp was on its feet, because we all felt that something tremendous was in the air. Rushing toward Gandhi's cot were the District Magistrate, the District Superintendent of Police, and about twenty armed policemen who watched us closely and kept their hands on revolvers. Directing a flashlight at Gandhi's face, they woke him up, and surrounded his cot, pressing us back. The Mahatma was told he was under arrest.

Calmly Gandhi asked if the magistrate would not be kind enough to read the warrant. This the magistrate did, in a trembling voice. Then Gandhi asked if he would be permitted to listen to his favorite hymn, one about the Ideal Man who is detached alike in bliss and sorrow. Permission was granted. When the singing was over, the Mahatma jumped up in a sprightly manner and rushed toward the waiting police lorry. When we asked him for a message for his wife, he smiled, and added, "She is a brave girl." In the dead of night, they stole him away.

But the movement went on, with increasing fury. There were acts of indiscretion, but there were few acts of violence on the people's part. Before the year was out, some hundreds were shot, and more than one hundred thousand, including twelve thousand Moslems, were imprisoned. The administration was at a standstill.

Realizing that India could not be quieted save through an understanding with the Congress, Lord Irwin released the leaders unconditionally on January 25, 1931, and opened negotiations.

. . . Gandhi had been going to the Viceregal Lodge since February 17. In fifteen days, Gandhi had visited the Viceroy's house some eight times, and now, on the night of March 4, the Mahatma and the Viceroy sat there, beaming like old estranged friends who have found a new understanding, their bitter struggle now belonging to the historic past. Gandhi guaranteed to call off his movement, while the Viceroy was prepared to declare a general amnesty, withdraw all emergency ordinances, allow peaceful picketing, rescind the government monopoly over the manufacture and sale of salt, and invite the Congress to a Round Table Conference in London in order to frame a new constitution for India.

Lord Irwin straightened his tall figure, smiled, and inquired whether the Mahatma would not pose with him for a picture to commemorate the occasion. This request was politely rejected by Gandhi on the ground that it was his principle never to pose for photographers. The Viceroy, still smiling, invited Gandhi for a spot of tea.

"Thank you," said Gandhi, unwrapping a paper parcel. "I shall put some of this legalized salt into my tea to remind us of the famous Boston Tea Party."

XIX. At the Round Table

*The earth is his bed, the vines are his pillow,
the sky is his roof, the winds are his fan, and the
moon is his lamp.*
                                        —Bhartrihari

*Nothing is more simple than greatness; indeed,
to be simple is to be great.*
                                        —Emerson

THE first-class cabins of
the *S. S. Rajputana*, on that voyage between Bombay
and England which commenced on August 29, 1931,
had lost their luster, while the third-class deck became
the center of attention. On his way to attend the Round
Table Conference in London, which had been called to
frame the new constitution for India, Gandhi did not
allow the royal invitation and mission to change his
mendicant ways. He was wont to travel third class in
India to share the hardships of the poorest of the poor.
The trip to London was being taken in behalf of these
same poor, and he could not adopt the ways of the more
fashionable leaders of India.

At Aden throngs of Arabs turned out to greet the Indian patriot. In Egypt he was hailed as "the great leader, Al Mahatma Gandhi," by Nahas Pasha, President of the Wafd Party. At Marseilles he was surrounded by the curious and welcomed by Western admirers.

He reached London on September 12, and parting company with his fellow delegates who had traveled in staterooms and who were headed for the Dorchester House or the Savoy, the Mahatma went directly to Kingsley Hall in East End where his pacifist friend, Muriel Lester, ran a neighborhood settlement for the poor industrial workers of the city. Was it not proper that a man "representing the poorest people of India should live among the poorest people of London" was the question behind the humble invitation of Kingsley Hall which had vied with the royal invitation and won out.

Fleet Street moved to the East End, for "Mr. Gandhi is the best news value in the world, always excepting of course the Prince of Wales." Soon fairy tales about Gandhi and his goat began to make headlines. George Slocombe wrote that Gandhi had prostrated himself before the Prince of Wales (the present Duke of Windsor) during the latter's visit to India. To this Gandhi took exception on the ground of poetic injustice. "I would bend the knee to the poorest scavenger, the poor untouchable in India, for having participated in crushing him for centuries. I would even take dust off his feet but I would not prostrate myself even before the King, much less before the Prince of Wales."

Invited to Buckingham Palace along with other dele-

gates to the Round Table Conference, the Mahatma appeared in his loincloth and chatted with King George V
and Queen Mary. Royalty was put at ease by Gandhi's
naturalness, while Kipling turned in his grave.

Bernard Shaw visited Gandhi. Emerging, he announced to the pressing reporters, with his usual modesty,
that he and Gandhi belonged to a very small minority in
the world. For "Gandhi is a man who comes once in a
thousand years." Charlie Chaplin went to see the
Mahatma. When the much-agitated secretary brought
the card bearing the famous name, Ghandi innocently
inquired who the distinguished visitor was; Gandhi had
never had time to see a movie. And when they met each
other, it was the Mahatma who kept the comedian
laughing.

The poor children of the East End began to flock
around Gandhi during his four-o'clock morning walks.
They found Gandhi to be a companion with hearty
humor instead of the austere old man they had imagined.
One boy wondered about the Mahatma's dress. Quickly,
he replied, "You in your country wear plus fours, I
prefer minus fours." The children laughed, and began to
call him "Uncle Gandhi." Fashionable women artists
who came to portray a shriveled-up ascetic envied his
"school-girlish complexion"—the result of his scientific
diet and regulated living.

Meanwhile, the Round Table Conference was for-
getting about Indian freedom and getting tangled up in
British constitutionalism. So Gandhi took a trip to Man-
chester, center of the textile industry. The British au-

thorities warned him against it as his boycotts were believed to be the cause of half of the unemployment in Lancashire. But instead of violence, Gandhi met with warm welcome, a tribute both to him and to the workers of England.

The Round Table Conference was a failure from the viewpoint of the Congress, whose sole representative Gandhi was. On his way back, he spent five days in Switzerland with Romain Rolland whose famous biography of Gandhi had first introduced the Indian Mahatma to Europe.

When he reached Bombay on December 28, the government had already struck at the Congress, behind his back, while he was negotiating with the British government in London. Expecting arrest, and explaining governmental repressions, Gandhi told a mammoth meeting in Bombay, "I take these as gifts from Lord Willingdon, our Christian Viceroy, for is it not a custom during Christmas to exchange greetings and gifts?"

XX. Too Many Births, Too Many Deaths

Population, when unchecked, increases in a geometrical ratio. Subsistence only increases in an arithmetical ratio.

—T. R. Malthus

The political problem of problems is how to deal with overpopulation, and it faces us on all sides.

—T. H. Huxley

ONE afternoon, five years later, during the heat wave of 1936, Gandhi gave a strange interview at his ashrama. The burning sun was acquiring a double shine on the silver stream of the Sabramati River below. On the roof of a simple house, in shade, sat the small, gaunt, dark man with a bandage of wet earth wrapped in white cloth around his head. There were four or five disciples around him, one fanning the meditative Mahatma.

This was the man of the East, Mahatma Gandhi, who had banished sex not only from his own life but who insisted that all physical relations between man and woman, save those between husband and wife for the express purpose of procreation, were ugly and evil.

Slowly ascending the stairs came the woman of the West, Margaret Sanger, who had, without intending to do so, freed sex to an extent hitherto unknown, and who had helped to create a society, again without intending to do so, wherein extra-marital relations were easy as well as fashionable.

She hesitated for a moment, perceiving that Gandhi had "an unusual light that shines in his face; that shines through the flesh; that circles around his head and neck like a mist with white sails of a ship coming through. It lasted only a few seconds, but it was there."

Breaking his usual custom, the Mahatma rose to greet the woman who typified so much of the West, turned his enchanting smile on a person he knew profoundly disagreed with him, accorded a warm welcome, and offered a seat.

Thus commenced one of the most incredible interviews of recent years.

No country can be free, said Mrs. Sanger, plunging headlong into the scheduled discussion, until its women acquire control over the power that is peculiarly theirs, the power of procreation. Unregulated fecundity meant overpopulation, poverty, strife, and war.

There was no quarrel so far. The Mahatma pointed out that all his life he had striven to make women conscious of their supreme role in society. "They have regarded me," added Gandhi, "as half woman because I have completely identified myself with them."

Too Many Births, Too Many Deaths

The example of Mrs. Gandhi seemed to offer a most glaring contradiction to this, and no one was more conscious of it than Gandhi himself. "I do not suppose," said Gandhi of his wife, "there are many women who can claim to have followed their husbands so slavishly as she has. She has followed, sometimes reluctantly, but her reluctance has had a tinge of obedience in it, for she is a good Hindu wife. I have often challenged her and asked to lead her own independent life but she will not do so. She is too much of a Hindu wife for that."

Indian poets have likened wives to the vines that twine themselves around the sturdy oaks. Manu, the law-giver, decreed that a woman could enter heaven only through the gate of her husband. Total and unflinching dedication to the husband and his work and his ideals has been the historic role of Hindu wives. This is not radically different from the social pattern that existed in Europe and even in America until recently. But the Western woman is emancipated now, and the Indian woman has made a start at breaking purdah. The numbers of emancipated Indian women are increasing by leaps and bounds.

Mrs. Gandhi continued to follow the old pattern, however. Apart from the hold that tradition had upon her, I suspect that in her decision to do so there was an awareness of her unique position; she knew that there was something worthy to follow in her husband. It is difficult but rewarding to be a wife of a genius; it is more difficult and more rewarding to be a wife of a saint who moves the multitudes.

[145]

When Gandhi decided to give away his earthly possessions, during his South African days, she offered up her personal jewelry to be distributed to the poor. When, about the same time, Gandhi decided to practice brahmacharya, or celibacy, she readily consented. In fact, in Gandhi's words, "There never was want of restraint on the part of my wife. Very often she would show restraint, but she rarely resisted me although she showed disinclination very often."

She took to his simple unseasoned and unspiced diet because Gandhi found it helped him control his passion. Born in comparative luxury, she did the housework because Gandhi did not believe in servants. And when Gandhi went to jail, so did she, again and again, until she died in jail by the side of her imprisoned hero. Women leaders like Mrs. Naidu have captured the imagination of the Indian people; Kasturbai Gandhi captured India's heart. And the affection between the two, husband and wife, became as inspiring as a folk song, shared by all.

Gandhi often succumbs to the idea that humanity is himself writ large. What was possible for him is possible for others, he thinks. "If I can drive home to women's minds the truth that they are free," said Gandhi to Mrs. Sanger, "we will have no birth control problem in India. If they will only learn to say 'no' to their husbands when they approach them carnally! The real problem is that they do not want to resist them."

Was the advocate of civil disobedience suggesting marital disobedience? In some states in America a wife has no right to resist her husband. India has no such laws, but Gandhi saw the necessity of mutual consent for a life of restraint. Marital maladjustment springing from sexless co-living can be avoided if there is mutual understanding.

When Mrs. Sanger made a distinction between sex love and sex lust, in the interest of artificial methods of birth control, Gandhi replied, "When both want to satisfy animal passion without having to suffer the consequences of their act, it is not love. It is lust. But if love is pure it will transcend animal passion and will regulate itself." Mrs. Sanger pointed out that Gandhi thought that all sexual acts save those for having children were immoral, and that if three children for each family were supposed to be enough, then there would possibly be only three sex acts in a couple's life. "How can you ask them," pleaded Mrs. Sanger, "who are so humble, so weak, to follow, when you who are so much stronger and wiser, have taken years to bring about that self-control in your life?"

Gandhi just smiled.

When Mrs. Sanger said that she believed in sex love, and that the more advanced the people the more evident is sex love, Gandhi asked, "May one man have pure sex love as distinguished from sex lust with more than one woman or a woman with more than one man? Your literature is full of that." Gandhi further reminded her that it was a real question, since polygamy is legal in India while in the West the law does not allow it.

Agreeing that the individual's control of sex is preferable to measures of birth control, Mrs. Sanger pointed out that many neurologists believed that continence caused mental disturbances in most cases. Gandhi retorted that their studies had been based on the examination of imbeciles. They should, instead, study healthy-minded people. Mrs. Sanger pointed out the contribution of the sex-act to the general health of the individual and to the increase of his vitality. Here Gandhi countered her most dogmatically, basing his assumptions on beliefs as old as the epic *Mahabharata*. Believing that it is the stored and controlled sexual fluid that gives vitality and energy to the individual, Gandhi objected to its dissipation. Gandhi is without knowledge of modern biochemistry which makes a distinction between male hormones and sexual cells.

Gandhi pointed out that in India it is not through the poor that the population increase comes. "Their lot is starvation," he added. "I have lived in it for twenty-one days, and I had no passion." It is the middle class that is running riot; otherwise, how would you have the low average of five children per family for India? And the middle class could be taught continence. He was not opposed to birth control, but to artificial means of controlling it. But he conceded that the case for artificial birth control was by no means weak, and it was because of this realization that he had given two days to this interview. He also confessed that great Indians like Tagore and Mrs. Naidu and Nehru were for it, though he himself considered it to be moral bankruptcy.

Margaret Sanger had her day, not with Gandhi, but

[148]

with India. The time was ripe. The problem was there, the overpowering problem of a teeming population. Within ten weeks she addressed forty public meetings, established about fifty centers of birth-control information. The All-India Women's Conference, more progressive than most women's organizations in the West, took up the cause of teaching artificial methods of birth control. So did the All-India Medical Conference, and Bombay Municipality.

When Margaret Sanger returned to the United States, she told me that she had more success in India in ten weeks than she had had in ten years in the United States. The political revolution has brought to India a spirit of readiness to change in other avenues of life. And there is no organized opposition to the movement, secular or religious.

Indian soil today sustains about one-fifth of the human race. The decennial census—the greatest adventure in census-taking in the world—of 1941 put the figure at 389 millions. It was 100 millions in the sixteenth century. It was 150 millions by the middle of the nineteenth century. It was 254 millions in 1881 when the first regular census was taken. It was 353 millions in 1931. The 1941 figure of 389 millions represents an increase of fifteen per cent over the period of the last ten years. At this rate, and if Margaret Sanger and her Hindu co-workers remain idle, Indians will be 700 million strong in 2001 A.D.

The fact that every ten years India is adding to its millions the population of an England, however, does not prove that Indian mothers hold a world record in fecundity. America beats India by one per cent in the rate of population increase.

Nor is India the most densely populated country in the world. The mean density for all India does not exceed 246 persons per square mile. This is nearly five and a half times the density of the United States. But England, Germany, Italy, Japan, Java, and Puerto Rico are more densely populated than India.

Some experts have calculated that India produces enough food for its vast population, and a little more. The chronic sub-starvation and periodic famines are caused by a faulty distribution system and by the vagaries of nature. But what is regarded as "enough" today for an Indian may not be the ideal standard for tomorrow. Standard of living is a relative term, and to increase it we will have to have a decrease in our birth rate to augment the blessings of greater production through expanded industries and scientific agriculture. Artificial birth control has come to stay in India, as in the West, in spite of Gandhi. As Bernard Shaw said, upon seeing Bombay for the first time, "I am struck by the fact that every man in Bombay is not a Mahatma."

XXI. The Hermitage

*It profiteth the Lord to have discreet shep-
herds, watchful and kindly, so that the sheep be
not tormented by their wrath but crop their pasture in peace and joyfulness; for it is a token of
the shepherd's kindness if the sheep be not scat-
tered abroad but browse around him in company.
Let him provide himself with a good barkable
dog and lie nightly with his sheep.*

—A Thirteenth-Century Treatise on
Estate Management

*For our humble woes and troubles
Rama hath the ready tear,
For our humble tales of suffering
Rama lends his willing ear!*

—The Ramayana

Edward Thompson, an-
other Westerner, finds Gandhi exasperating because the
Mahatma might send a telegram that would bring a
friend or colleague hundreds of miles clear across the
subcontinent, on some presumably important matter,
only to terminate the discussion and use up what might

be the only time available "because the exact minute has arrived when he gives his patients enemas!"

Edward Thompson is not alone among Gandhi's Western friends and admirers to call Gandhi, affectionately, "a bit trying." Clare Sheridan, famous sculptress and a cousin of Winston Churchill, was allowed to model his portrait only after the following admonition, "I cannot pose; you must let me go on with my work, and do the best you can." Gandhi is against posing on principle. He will never sit still or assume an attitude even for a camera snapshot.

No false modesty is involved here. Immortalization of his physical likeness is just not important to him. In fact it is impertinent. There are thousands of his photographs, but never has he been known to designate one as his favorite. But to go back to Clare Sheridan—after days of work, during which Gandhi received many visitors, from the Archbishop of Canterbury to the Aga Khan, when she asked Gandhi what he thought of the finished head, he simply replied, "I do not know. I cannot judge of my own face, and I know nothing about art—but you have worked well!" And yet she and another sculptor, Jo Davidson, agree that compared to Gandhi most of the prominent men of our time "were disappointing to meet," and that the only other man to leave an equally deep impression upon them was Lenin.

Gandhi has a habit of granting interviews to foreign correspondents in the wee hours of morning, at four or five, when he regularly takes his daily walk. It would seem as though the impish ascetic liked to have his fun at the expense of those who, often enough, dissipate their best working hours in night clubs. But that is not the case. To have a press, or even a good press, is not important to Gandhi. He abhors publicity and propaganda.

He was the first to induce the Congress Party to close all its foreign offices on the grounds that good work done at home and strength developed within the country will not long pass unnoticed. Seeing the representatives of the press he regards as a necessary evil of modern civilization and, as such, a relatively unimportant thing. So he gives them the least important hours of his daily round—hours devoted to physical survival and not to the ennobling of the soul.

Some of his Indian colleagues also consider that he fritters away his energies in trivialities. For instance, he will keep even men like Nehru and Khan waiting while he analyzes the bad dreams of one of his pupils or discusses the ideal thickness of soup with those conducting the community kitchen. But Gandhi is an artist of life who knows how to distinguish between a minor detail and a trivial one. It is only through attention to minor but important details, he contends, that men can make sweeping but sound judgements. Westerners like General Montgomery would take a diametrically opposite view and say that important men making important decisions must be spared the burden of commonplace routine. But it is apt to be in the little things of life that man finds inspiration.

A touching description revealing the "wholeness" of Gandhi's intimate life is provided by Mahadev Desai, who had made Gandhi a most fortunate man in Tagore's estimation, "for the Mahatma had the ideal secretary." Gandhi's Boswell depicts a typical day in Gandhi's life at his hermitage near Wardha in the Central Provinces. It is called Sevagram, or "Serviceville." Gandhi sometimes jestingly calls it a "Home for the Invalids," even a "lunatic asylum." Gandhi says that he can draw his inspiration only from his natural setting. He is happiest among his patients, both physical and mental. He is a healer. Because Gandhi is primarily concerned with his patients—those who depend on him—even while away, his comrades in the Congress high command hold most of their meetings at Sevagram, so as not to take the Mahatma away from the highland of his heart. The late Lord Lothian and Sir Stafford Cripps went to see Gandhi there in order to understand him better.

Gandhi's is the smallest mud hut in a colony of mud huts and thatched roofs. To a Hindu even godliness is next to cleanliness, and so the hut is immaculate. Save for the palm-leaf mats, there is hardly any furniture in it, and only occasionally are low stools provided for Westerners who cannot squat as cross-legged as Buddha without cramping their joints. The walls are decorated with mud reliefs done by Miraben, daughter of an English admiral.

This small sitting room is turned into a dining room at 11:00 A.M. punctually every day. All of Gandhi's current patients must be fed in his presence in strict observance of his instructions. Immediately after the meal, Gandhi goes through his voluminous mail and daily papers, and then takes his siesta, the only concession he makes to India's ill-fated laziness. Like Napoleon he falls asleep at a moment's notice, and wakes up at the decided time, to the minute, without outside help.

Then starts his endless string of interviews and conferences. Most of the time he reclines, with a mud poultice on his abdomen, his own prescription for high blood pressure. For this purpose he prefers the Indian earth of which he is made. Some "correct" Englishmen do resent his not standing up to receive his guests, especially ladies, but in the first place, Indian etiquette does not require him to stand and, in the second place, the guest is invariably accorded a more genuine welcome and a more cordial greeting than etiquette would permit. In the third place, a mortal man has only a limited amount of energy. As between being correct and useful, Gandhi has decided upon the latter.

With religious regularity, an hour is devoted to spinning. To Gandhi, the spinning-wheel is both the symbol of his village reconstruction movement and an economic solvent for agrarian India. At five comes the final meal of the day, dates and nuts and curd. Then follows his evening walk. Quite often he utilizes it for his play with the children of Sevagram, who are perhaps his greatest source of delight and relaxation.

"Bapuji," asks the little grandson, "you are going to Delhi?"

"Yes."

"Why?"

"To see the Viceroy."

"But you always go to see the Viceroy. Why does not the Viceroy come to see you?" Everyone laughs, but Gandhi's laughter is the heartiest and most childlike.

The evening prayers are participated in by all members, and by people coming from surrounding villages. There in the middle sits Gandhi, his head, with its un-Indian baldness, shining in the twilight, his eyes closed, his legs crossed, his spinal cord erect as a staff. First there is chanting of Sanskrit verses from *The Bhagavad Gita*, the description of the Ideal Man. Then there is singing by the musician of a devotional song. Then there is a dhoon, or the constant and rapid repetition of a couplet by the congregation, intoxicating as a jungle drum. At the end Gandhi delivers a sermon, which can be on any subject from the illness of a member or a mistake of his wife's, to an announcement that he is about to launch a nation-wide struggle against the British. Here it is that the reporters can come closest to what goes on in Gandhi's bald head.

Gandhi prefers to sleep on a cot out in the open or on a verandah. Years of imprisonment have taught him the art of star-gazing, and he has made quite a study of heavenly phenomena. Only an Indian can understand the joy of looking up to the stars, lying on his back, and listening to the music of silence such as one hears sometimes on a secluded mountain top.

Gandhi gets up before the birds, at three, and concludes his thinking and reading while everything else is serene and quiet. (My own experience both at his university and at Tagore's school, called The Abode of

The Hermitage

Peace, is that those dream hours are the most conducive to creative thought.) Then he goes methodically, like a Brahmin, through the daily ablutions without which a Hindu cannot touch any food. The morning prayer over, he takes his meager breakfast, and then a morning walk, the nightmare of visiting foreigners who do not relish it but who cannot bear the thought of being left out of what is reported to be Gandhi's most intimate hour.

Originally Sevagram was designed to meet Gandhi's need for solitude, and all were to be barred including Mrs. Gandhi. But Gandhi has no heart to say "no" in personal matters. It was thus that the cycle of the hermit's story started. The hermit had a cat; a cow was needed to provide milk; a cowherd to tend to the cow, and so on. Now Sevagram has a dairy on the grounds, gardens for vegetables and cereals, a dispensary, a school, and offices of various organizations connected with village advancement.

Gandhi is very loyal to old co-workers and friends, and Sardar Patel, who plays Stalin to Gandhi's Lenin, describes Sevagram as a "menagerie." One of its inhabitants is Professor Bhansali, who was once a brilliant teacher at the national university in Ahmedabad. He went to jail several times in accordance with the fortunes of the Gandhi movement. Then he turned a recluse, holding an All-India, if not All-World, record for fasting. Next, he took to the woods and wandered for years completely nude, without shoes or a light in places swarming with scorpions and snakes. (For

weren't animals his brothers as much as human beings!)
He believed in silence to establish harmony with eternity; so he sewed up his lips with a copper ring. He
would eat only raw wheat flour and neem leaves, which
are bittersweet.

He stumbled upon Gandhi once more and the latter
persuaded him to wrap a loincloth around his waist so
that he could live in the community. The Professor was
opposed to work on philosophic grounds, but Gandhi
converted him to the dignity of labor, and now he cards
and weaves and spins for seventeen hours a day. But he
somehow manages to keep his neighbors nervous.

In his mud hut, Gandhi might be sitting in conference
with Nehru and other party dignitaries, or with Sir
Stafford Cripps and his staff. In would rush Professor
Bhansali, agitated. All business is abandoned.

"I remember to have lied once five years ago," says
the Professor to the Mahatma. "I must go through some
fiery penance in atonement. Will you please give me
permission to hang myself down our well head-over-
heels for five hours?"

The question of cooperation with the British during
World War II, or of a general strike as the alternative,
would have to await a more propitious moment when
the Mahatma would have time for such matters. At present he must spend two hours in dissuading Professor
Bhansali from taking such an uncalled-for somersault.
And that is just what the Mahatma proceeds to do, while
his colleagues stare, speechless, or leave silently one by
one.

The Hermitage

A Japanese monk was another member of Gandhi's group. Every morning and evening he would go about the colony merrily beating his drum and chanting Buddhist prayers that Japan had learned from China, and China from India. In between times he would work hard at anything the small community needed. He believed in the Japanese mission in China, and the British, during the war, took advantage of the fact to say that Gandhi harbored a Japanese spy.

A man who had got leprosy while he was in prison with Gandhi, a great Sanskrit scholar, wandered away for years as a castaway and fasted occasionally in advanced stages of the disease. One morning he came back to Gandhi.

"How can I say 'no' to you?" said Gandhi. "Who will look after you if I don't? I shall build you a hut beside my own, and you will make the place your abode. Even if no one else remains here, you at least shall stay."

Gandhi sees the leper every day while at Sevagram, and sometimes worships him by taking the dust off his feet as a token of his reverence for the sick man's learning. There is a touch of the Nazarene in this twentieth-century healer who also is a leader of man.

Maurice Frydman, an engineer of genius and a restless spirit, a refugee from Hitler's tyranny, went to Mysore in South India and began to make a fortune. Soon, however, he came in contact with Ramana Maharshi, who never leaves his abode but whose fame has traveled throughout India and as far West as France. W. Somerset Maugham told me that he had never before experienced such tranquillity of mind as he did in the presence of Ramana Maharshi; and the silent teacher of the hero of *The Razor's Edge* has been drawn after Ramana Maharshi. The Maharshi, or the Great Saint, does not converse with you, nor does he give you any advice. His is a face of silence. Hundreds have testified that to be in the Maharshi's presence is an uplifting experience, as it is to be in Gandhi's presence. With this difference, however; the Mahatma is a karmayogi, or a yogi through great deeds, while the Maharshi is a dhyanayogi, or a yogi through contemplation.

Converted by the Maharshi's silence, Frydman went to the little Mahatma, who is busy as a bee and whose hours of contemplation are by necessity few and far between. Nowadays Frydman, a product of Western science and a master of modern technology, believes utterly in the gospel of cottage crafts and the culture that is based upon agriculture and a village life close to nature.

A princess also dwells in Gandhi's motley colony. Her name is Rajkumari Amrit Kaur. She has given up her worldly state and become one of the several secretaries of the Mahatma.

To this constellation of mud huts and bamboo mattings, amidst this group of people which represents all the nuances from the ridiculous to the sublime, are brought India's most pressing problems by men who are the molders of that country. And it is here, too, that Westerners interested in Gandhi, and governments embroiled in Indian politics, make their inevitable trek.

The Hermitage

Should this be the pattern of a public man's life! Westerners naturally wonder. Should a man who holds India's destiny in the hollow of his wasted palm allow himself to be encumbered by all the details of running a primitive boarding house? Is it not the antithesis of the Western notion of efficiency? How can a man be a specialist—and specialists are supposed to be the most useful of people—while he fritters away his time and energy in experiments not in one field but in all fields of life and afterlife? Gandhi not only puts a limit to his own efficiency by his limitless interests, he also blunts the efficiency of those who must deal with him. He becomes comparatively unapproachable to those who are his colleagues as well as his opponents in politics. His thinking becomes remote from the understanding of those who have accepted the modern notion of specialization. Gandhi had to rush back to the sick people of Sevagram even while Sir Stafford Cripps was conducting fateful negotiations at Delhi. British statesmen could not see him in 1931 during the Round Table Conference because he was busy discussing the divinity of Christ with the dignitaries of the Church of England. Was Gandhi a statesman, on a decisive political mission, or was he merely an unusual showman, asked the doubting Thomases. Cannot some of the appalling shortcomings in Gandhi's political dealings be ascribed to his temptation to be a master of many trades?

The neat notion of efficiency here confronts the massive but none too well-defined pattern of greatness. One is efficient at a certain time in a given area; one is great independent of time and space. A great man is a whole man. Not only he is a member of society; he is a link in the history of man. He is something more. He is himself. In the presence of God, no other capacity counts save that of being oneself. There are artists of genius, who are not great men. There are towering statesmen, who are not great men. These are gifted men who have become experts in particulars. Gandhi is essentially a whole man, and only secondarily a statesman, a revivalist, and a social reformer. His basic interest is the art of living and of dying and of maintaining an evolutionary trend through that cycle which ends in godhead. Uplifting the poverty-stricken Indians, giving a sense of self-respect to the politically exploited, battling against imperial arrogance and tyranny, are important because it is through such channels that his soul can seek expansion during this life which is bounded by the time of the twentieth century and by the space, primarily, of India. Nothing pertaining to man, therefore, is alien to Gandhi.

Nirvana, preoccupation of Indian sages from time immemorial, is regarded by some Christian scholars as a particularly selfish end, placing individual welfare ahead of the common weal. But this would be only when both ends had a mundane frame of reference. Salvation of individual solitude is not to be identified with worldly interests of a being. Salvation of the soul is a spiritual concept, and it is attained through the media of services to mankind. Service of humanity is thus transformed from a moral gratification into a personal obligation.

The all-embracing sweep of awareness exhibited in a

great life should include the joys and pleasure of living as well. And it does. It is in this light that Gandhi's conspicuous asceticism acquires a new meaning. It is on the note of happiness that his life revolves; the difference between him and a hedonist is to be found in the levels and intensity of happiness, and not in Gandhi's mortification of the body. Catholic scholasticism has already conveyed this idea, in scientific terminology, to the Western world. The height of happiness is in inverse ratio to the rapidity of satiety. The pleasure of eating ice cream is short-lived compared to that of looking at a sunset, which in turn is of short duration in comparison to the joy of loving a son. The more removed is the pleasure from the gratification of the senses, the more lasting it is. Abstract experience is independent of the ups and downs of sensual satisfactions. Thus we resolve the seeming conflict between the otherworldly salvation of religions like Hinduism and Christianity, on one hand, and the worldly utilitarianism of Bentham and Mill. In this light the principle of the greatest happiness for the greatest number, or of the greatest number of happy peoples, will serve not only as a basis for global unity between peoples and cultures, but also as a basis for unity between soul and society. It should be remembered in this connection that Gandhi and the monks were not born in monasteries.

The peculiar genius of Indian culture has lent force to the wholeness of life exemplified by Gandhi. The famous Swiss psychologist Jung, disciple of Freud, was struck in India by this phenomenon. India today represents not merely a stage in cultural development; it displays all the stages in the march of civilization at the same time. The Hindus have a way of preserving the most primitive by the side of the most highly developed. With the crude animal sacrifice on the altar of Kali is coupled a theory of shakti, or energy, that is suitable for the atomic age. For not all of the souls, who are marching toward their respective salvations, but who are caught within a synchronization of time and space ("in our time"), are uniform in their development. They are on the same path, but they move between different milestones. A complete life, therefore, takes into account all stages of evolution of all men.

The contrast between the complete view of life and the specialized view of life is nowhere so acute as in the treatment of the madman. Modern psychiatrists have identified mental disease with the failure to make adjustment in a given cultural milieu. Insanity thus becomes a disease more social than syphilis; the latter is contagious and not social at all. Insanity is a personality disease, and personality is a social concept. It arises somewhere between the society and the individual in the process of becoming a person. Maladjustments in a given culture, or falling below the norm accepted by a society, are personality lags but not individual blemishes. And we cannot be sure that it is the person at fault and not the culture. For there can be nothing but perfection when man is conceived. At that moment soul assumes a body and from that time begins the process of personality formation in a given society. Sanity or insanity, normal-ity or abnormality, develop after that beginning and have little bearing on the march of the individual solitude toward cosmic awareness. That is why a village madman is as integral a part of a rural Indian community as the village moneylender. That is why a "touched" person has a place in Gandhi's scheme of things.

XXII. "Quit India!"

>   . . . Grandsires, sires and sons,
> Brothers, and fathers-in-law, and sons-in-law,
> Elders and friends! Shall I deal death on these
> Even though they seek to slay us? Not one blow,
> O Madhusudan! will I strike to gain
> The rule of the Three Worlds; then, how much less
> To seize an earthly Kingdom! Killing these
> Must breed but anguish, Krishna! If they be
> Guilty, we shall grow guilty by their deaths;
> Their sins will light on us, if we shall slay
> Those sons of Dritirashtra, and our kin;
> What peace could come of that, O Madhava?
> For if indeed, blinded by lust and wrath,
> These cannot see, or will not see, the sin
> Of Kingly lines o'erthrown and kinsmen slain,
> How should not we, who see, shun such a crime—
> We who perceive the guilt and feel the shame.
>
> —The Bhagavad Gita

> The politics of those whose goal is beyond time
> are always pacific; it is the idolators of past and
> future, of reactionary memory and Utopian
> dream, who do the persecuting and make the
> wars.
>
> —Aldous Huxley

> One cause is good
> Until the other's understood.
> —Poor Robin's Almanac

[166]

"Quit India!"

FOR a few years tranquil Sevagram remained the center of what Gandhi calls his "constructive program." But once again the Mahatma was catapulted to the center of the national struggle which raged within the global holocaust of World War II. Leaving his usual peaceful rural surroundings, he returned to a city which had seen some of his greatest battles.

The city of Bombay, after experiencing an unusual wave of jubilation and fighting fervor, lay in the quiet of the exhausted in the early hours of August 9, 1942. One by one the municipal lamps along the sloping thoroughfares of Malabar Hill were going out so as not to look pitiable in the morning light slowly coming up from behind the eastern hills. But one lamp kept burning in a sumptuous mansion on the hill crest; for Gandhi sat there drafting his last appeals to the Viceroy, to President Roosevelt, to Generalissimo Chiang Kai-shek, and to Ivan Maisky, Soviet Ambassador to the Court of St. James.

On the previous day he had electrified the masses attending the momentous August 8th Meeting of the All-India Congress Committee by unequivocally demanding that the British "Quit India." His slogan was "Karenge ya Marenge"—Do or Die. He had, however, cautioned his followers that it would be weeks before a civil disobedience movement could be launched. First, he wanted to write a letter to the Viceroy asking for an interview with the object of seeking a peaceful solution. And he also wanted to appeal to the Big Three—United States, Russia, and China—to arbitrate a dispute embroiling the Big Fourth—Britain. So, when the tumult and the shouting subsided, he quietly withdrew to his room in the Birla House to formulate his final appeals, his believing heart at rest, confident that an open break, if any, was not in the stars of that night.

There was commotion in the courtyard. Soon there was a knock at his door. The representatives of law and order were there to inform him that he was under arrest, and that he was to be confined in the so-called Aga Khan Palace. The government had moved swiftly, struck throughout the entire country, and imprisoned hundreds of Congress leaders during the same night.

The nation was stunned and leaderless. In a day or two it recovered from the shock and struck back with blind fury, without the benefit of any guidance from its tried leaders who had been rounded up overnight. Their pent-up resentment ran amuck and broke the bounds of Gandhian non-violence. There followed weeks and months of violent outbreaks which convulsed the country and paralyzed the war effort. There followed the raging retaliation by the government whose force matched that used during the aftermath of the so-called Sepoy Mutiny.

No other action had cost Gandhi so many Western friends. No other action of the British Government of India had made India more disillusioned about the West.

But the white fury of war cannot be understood save in the light of events that led up to it. . . .

In February, 1937, the first provincial elections were held under the new 1935 Constitution hammered out during the Round Table Conferences. The Congress Party swept the polls, came into power in eight out of the eleven provinces, and formed the largest single blocs, though not absolute majorities, in the remaining three. The London *Times* commented: "The Congress Party alone is organized on more than a provincial basis. The party has won its victories . . . on issues which interested millions of Indian rural voters and scores of millions who had no votes."

When the Congress decided to assume office in July, Gandhi set the pattern of the new ministers; they were to be "honest, selfless, industrious, vigilant, and solicitous for the true welfare of the starving millions." In consequence, even a prime minister of a province like Madras was to forego his sumptuous salary, guaranteed in the new constitution, and accept only five hundred rupees (around two hundred dollars) per month. Several provincial ministers had to find time from their busy schedules to go out and teach school gratis daily in connection with the campaign to eradicate illiteracy from India. The ministers were to lead a life of service, like so many carbon-copy Mahatmas.

The Congress cabinets in the various provinces concentrated on prohibition, relief of peasantry, basic free and compulsory education, labor legislation, Hindu-Moslem unity by control of communal riots, and removal of untouchability by opening Hindu temples to the "pariahs." They made so much progress during the brief period they were in power that English statesmen and periodicals, both in India and England, had nothing but praise for them.

But the satisfactory fulfillment of public expectations was offset by inner difficulties. The Congress had achieved success through non-violence. But now it had assumed the functions of a government, which included policing and punishing lawbreakers. The former self-styled civil lawbreakers, now in positions of power, had to use police and magisterial violence to curb riots and control labor disputes. The tables were turned even on Gandhi, who had refused to accept any official position. A group of untouchables went to his Sevagram center and started a fast in Mrs. Gandhi's hut in protest against the Mahatma. The dispute was amicably settled, proving the point that such technique as fast and non-violence can be effective only if truth and justice are on your side. Gandhi, however, was alert enough to perceive the dilemma of erstwhile non-violent rebels who were now in charge of law and order and who were finding it difficult to maintain them without recourse to force. Always a purist, Gandhi ascribed the self-contradiction not to the principle of non-violence, but to its inadequate understanding by the ministers of his party.

The Congress was a revolutionary party until it assumed office. The techniques of rebels are different from those of statesmen, and sometimes the best way to break a radical is to give him power. There is a further revolu-

tionary dilemma involved when revolutionists subscribe
to the strategy of grabbing whatever power is offered
them and then asking for more. During periods of
collaboration, the edge of their revolutionary ardor is
apt to be dulled and blunted. Nehru wrote to Gandhi in
a heart-searching mood that the Congress ministers were
"trying to adapt business far too much to the old order
and trying to justify it. . . . We are apt to be misled by
the illusion that we possess power."

Apart from these inner philosophic conflicts, the Congress ministries were rendering evident public service.
Even a Tongawallah who drove a coach-and-two held
his head high because it was "his government," made
possible by his vote. All ex-jail-birds, the Congress
ministers were quite anxious to turn jails into reforma-
tories, and quite a few jailors were thanking their stars
they had not treated their present masters too roughly
when they had been their wards. The pattern of the
Englishman's relations with the Indian was also changing. The word "native" was banished from official vo-
cabulary by law, and arrogant White Sahibs of yesterday now had to wait in the antechambers of Indian
ministers under whom they served.

As the Indian sky was becoming brighter, the storm
was gathering over Europe. Gandhi was against the
Czech surrender which came in October, 1938. Offering
Dr. Benes a weapon "not of the weak but of the brave,"
Gandhi suggested that "unarmed men, women and children offering non-violent resistance without any bitterness in them will be novel experience" for the tyrants.

Anyway, the alternative was Munich, commenting on which Gandhi affirmed, "I suggest that if it is brave, as it is, to die to a man fighting against odds, it is braver still to refuse to fight and yet refuse to yield to the usurpers."

In the December, 1938, with war clouds gathering both in the East and the West, Takaoka, member of the Japanese Diet, visited Gandhi at Segaon with a view to appraising the Mahatma. To his overtures, Gandhi flatly replied, "I do not subscribe to the doctrine of Asia for the Asiatics, if it is meant as an anti-European combination."

The Congress movement for freedom in British India was now augmented by a drive for representative government in the Native States. The year 1939 will go down in Indian history as the beginning of the "Yellow Revolution." The map of India is printed in two inks, pink signifying British India, while the yellow dots mark Indian States; hence the name, "Yellow Revolution." The Maharajahs, like the feudal lords of medieval Europe, were regarded as anachronisms in an India marching toward democracy. They had to go or be content with the status of constitutional monarchs, like the King of England. There was no halfway house between their complete disappearance and representative government in their domains. Making a test case of the Thakore of Rajkot, whose sires had been served by Gandhi's own, the Mahatma went on a fast on March 3, against what he described as the "wanton breach, instigated by the British Resident in Rajkot," of the charter of liberty. Within four days, at the suggestion of the Viceroy, the

ruler agreed to arbitration and the fast was broken. Sir
Maurice Gwyer, Chief Justice, gave a decision favorable
to Gandhi's claims.

Gandhi's revival of the institution of willing suffering
as a means of reconciliation and atonement now seems
as out-of-place and impracticable to modern men as it
did to the Romans, who, in nailing Christ to a cross,
thought merely to rid themselves of another agitator.
What was good for an Indian Hitler seemed good for a
German autocrat. In July, the Mahatma wrote an open
letter to Hitler, asking the dictator to desist from plunging the world into war. Perhaps Gandhi was a fool, but a
God's Fool, who regards no one as utterly lost because
man is a reflection of the divine and as such susceptible
to regeneration under all circumstances.

Cognizant of the approaching crisis, the Congress
made its position clear, so that there would be no mis-
understanding later, in a resolution dated August 12:
"In this world crisis the sympathies of the Working
Committee are entirely with the peoples who stand for
democracy and freedom and the Congress has repeatedly
condemned fascist aggression in Europe, Africa, and the
Far East of Asia. . . . The Congress has further clearly
enunciated its policy in the event of war and declared
its determination to oppose all attempts to impose a war
on India." Subsequent Congress acts or failures to act
during World War II should have been judged in the
light of this resolution.

But within a few short hours of England's declaration
of war against Germany on September 3, the Viceroy

committed India's 389,000,000 people to war without so much as a by-your-leave from its representative ministers. The nationalists contended that it was morally wrong to plunge millions of Indians into a bloody war without assessing their will. The British contended that they were legally correct in assuming that His Majesty's Indian "subjects," not being free citizens of the self-governing dominions, were automatically at war whenever their English sovereign was at war. Again it was a conflict between a moral code and a legal code. The provincial ministries formed by the Congress resigned in protest on November 8, announcing that "Co-operation must be between equals by mutual consent for a cause which both consider to be worthy. . . . India cannot associate herself in a war said to be for democratic freedom when that very freedom is denied to her." The government invoked Section 93, suspended the new constitution in the Congress provinces, and ordered British governors to rule by fiat.

This action was later held as a tactical blunder on the part of the Congress, even by some of the friends of India's freedom. They argued that in so doing the Congress bade good-bye to whatever little democratic influence it had over the country and gave a free rein to reactionary forces. The Congress should have hung on to its power, they added, and made the best of a bad bargain.

To most Englishmen and their allies, to most Americans, especially after Pearl Harbor (to take the most charitable view), this action of the Gandhi party meant shirking in face of duty, and a national inability to comprehend common danger. To the West, galvanized by catastrophe, civilization itself was in danger if Nazi hordes went unchecked. Even India's freedom was at stake; for in a Fascist world the freedom to demand freedom would not be allowed.

To Indians (again to take the most charitable view), this sounded like a piece of crisis-thinking. Neither England nor the United States could be completely absolved from building up Germany and Japan at a time when the Indian National Congress sided with democratic forces in Ethiopia, in Spain, in China, in Czechoslovakia. Maybe Britain and America came to recognize the Fascist monster late in the day, but India had recognized it long ago and she had been frustrated in her attempts to combat it. India, in her own quiet way, had been fighting against a form of Fascism for more than two hundred years. For the only difference between Fascism and Imperialism is that the former functions also at home.

The Indian trend of thought, however, was open to the Western charge of being purist and perfectionist. (But all action would have to cease, in the light of such thinking, for man shall always be imperfect.) Even Western liberals, "knights in rusty armor," who had thus far been supporters of the Indian view, began to be critical. They had been on the losing side for so long that now they were eager to be on the winning side and ready to make a common cause with the Conservatives against Fascism. They insisted that Indians like the rest should discriminate between higher values and lower values, recognize the difference between the Small Evil and the Great Evil, and take up a sword against the Great Evil in order to gain time to combat later the Small Evil.

The Indian mind wondered. Were the latter-day crusaders glowing with eternal virtues or crisis-virtues? How could you regard, the thinking Indian asked, freedom from Germany as different from freedom from England, freedom from Fascism as different from freedom from Imperialism? How can slaves fight for someone else's freedom? Would their chains allow them to act?

At this point, the latter-day Western crusader looked with pity mingled with sympathy at the immobile mystic. An adept at specialized thinking, he implied that you could not achieve anything in this world unless you defined your problem, limited its ramifications, and then concentrated on its solution. There is a strength in this, but it is a power the philosopher, with his universal thought, lacks. The paramount problem was Hitler and what he stood for. If you got entangled in larger issues, the Evil One would not give you a second chance to make up your mind.

The Hindu mind smiled tolerantly. If the Westerner was logical, the Indian was cosmological. The Indian refused to think of Fascism in isolation. To him the question was between the tyrant and the free but weak man. The battle must be fought on that fundamental level, wherever that problem existed. Democracy's first victory, in consequence, was to be won in India. Only then Indians would be able to fight tyranny and injustice as represented by Hitler and the Mikado.

If India was unique (to take the most philosophical view) in the modern world, Gandhi was unique even in India. His was a greatness which stamps infinity on the thoughts of men. Periodic battles against ill-defined and recurring and varying manifestations of Evil must be replaced by the fight against Evil itself. Wars, at best, have staved off immediate national annihilations but have not halted mankind in its inexorable march toward total extinction. And so the great argument went on . . .

On July 2, Gandhi issued his famous appeal "To Every Briton" to accept the method of non-violent resistance even against Hitler, thus bringing on himself the ridicule that men generally heap on a man who abides by eternal verities in fair weather or foul. Prophets have never tired of telling the world that truth triumphs eventually, and the world has never failed to repudiate them. In the past it did so by ignoring prophetic insight and calling it impracticable. But modern civilization is different. Its secularism is conscious and defined and even aggressive. It is not abashed, as were the past ages, in affirming the new religion of social effectiveness. Wrote John Stuart Mill, one of the rationalizers of the modern age: "The dictum that truth always triumphs over persecution is one of those pleasant falsehoods which men repeat after one another till they pass into commonplaces but which all experience refutes. History teems with instances of truth put down by persecution.

If not suppressed forever, it may be thrown back for centuries. . . . Persecution has always succeeded, save where the heretics were too strong a party to be effectively persecuted. It is a piece of idle sentimentality that truth, merely as truth, has any inherent power denied to error, of prevailing against the dungeon and the stake. Men are not more zealous for truth than they often are for error, and a sufficient application of legal or even of social penalities will generally succeed in stopping the propagation of either."

Perhaps modern man knows better. Mill goes on: "The real advantage which truth has consists in this, that when an opinion is true, it may be extinguished once, twice, or many times, but in the course of ages there will generally be found persons to rediscover it, until some one of its reappearances falls on a time when from favorable circumstances it escapes persecution until it has made such head as to withstand all subsequent attempts to suppress it." That, then, is the central issue between the Mahatma and the world. The modern man is too impatient. He wants results immediate enough to be enjoyed in his lifetime. For this he is ready to employ any means that he thinks will be effective. For he is preoccupied (to draw upon a recurrent theme in this book because it is also a recurrent note in Gandhi's life) with his horizontal existence, with himself with a name in a given country, also named, and within the span of his life. To the Mahatma, on the other hand, this life is only a phase of the life eternal, and the horizontal is for the edification of the vertical drive toward godhead to which all creation aspires. The means, therefore, are inseparable from the end; they are the end in the making. As the modern man is open to the charge of being oblivious of the everlasting, so the Mahatma is open to the charge of being oblivious of the immediate. This is another way of saying that men like Gandhi are invariably too far ahead of their times. In Mill's phraseology, Mahatmas generally confuse "just any circumstance" with "favorable circumstance" for the vindication of truth.

The Mahatma's inflexibility could not be emulated even by his Indian colleagues who too felt harried by the impact of the war. The time invariably comes when Mahatmas become too much. After the fall of France, on June 20, the Working Committee of the Congress, foreseeing that the use of physical force might become imperative in the national interest, resolved that "The problem of the achievement of national freedom has now to be considered along with the allied one of its maintenance and the defense of the country against possible external aggression and internal disorder," and that the Congress was "free to take political decisions without having to think of their implications in terms of violence and non-violence." The resolution went on to absolve Gandhi of any responsibility. Explained Nehru: "Gandhiji felt, and probably rightly, that he could not give up or tone down a message which he had for the world. He must have freedom to give it as he liked and not be kept back by political exigencies. So for the first time, he went one way and the Congress Working Committee another."

Gandhi was more than willing to stand aside if the majority of his Congress colleagues felt that violence had to be used. As he cherished his mission of non-violence, so also he respected the processes of democracy wherein the majority decides. And a great change had come over the Congress mentality after Pearl Harbor. Now America was at war, a country whom the Congressmen regarded as a friend as well as a Galahad and after whose War of Independence their own movement was patterned. Congress leaders were anxious to make a common cause with the United States, and incidentally with Britain, on terms of armed resistance against the Axis. Perceiving this change in his co-workers, Gandhi smiled a saintly smile, and addressed the Working Committee meeting at Bardoli on December 30: "Ahimsa [non-violence] with me is a creed, the breath of my life. But it is never as a creed that I placed it before India, or for that matter before anyone except in casual informal talks. I placed it before the Congress as a political method, to be employed for the solution of political questions. . . . As a political method, it can always be changed, modified, altered, even given up in preference to another. . . . If you can get what you want, you will strike the bargain, and you may be sure that I will not shed a single tear."

This distinction between Ends and Means which Gandhi permitted his followers, and which he would not allow himself, became of paramount importance in the light of a subsequent controversy. Neither the rejection of the Cripps offer, nor the refusal to participate in the war until India was independent, was caused by Gandhian inhibitions of non-violence. Congress was ready to take up arms against Germany and Japan on condition that India was first recognized as a free and equal partner. On the crucial issue of Satyagraha, the Congress had parted company with Gandhi, while ever appreciating the Mahatma's personal steadfastness to his ideal.

When Sir Stafford Cripps pressed Gandhi to see him on March 27, Gandhi was not even a "four-anna member" of the Congress. He was unwilling to participate in the negotiations, but he could not resist the invitation of an old admirer who was also a vegetarian like himself, a reported ascetic, and a friend of India.

Describing the Cripps offer as "a post-dated cheque," Gandhi in one phrase summed up India's objection to the eleventh-hour Coalition effort. According to the Congress view, there were plenty of promises in it to be redeemed at the successful conclusion of the war, but there was little in it which could satisfy India's desire to be an equal partner in a crusade they wanted to make their own. For the duration of the war, India was largely to continue as she was. Especially in the military field, there was to be no change, and in wartime there is no authority but military authority. From the British point of view, Churchill had gone as far as he could under war conditions wherein any fundamental constitutional change was unthinkable.

Gandhi did not stay in New Delhi to await the outcome of the Cripps negotiations, which eventually failed. Armed as they are with the enviable advantage of hindsight, an advantage never available to the men who must make the decisions at a given moment, many well-wishers of India have regretted the Congress intransigence which, by the way, was shared by all the parties of India. In the Congress rejection of the Cripps offer they perceived the incapability of the revolutionary who, in search of a perfect denouement, fails to take an opportunity which alone can make a perfect ending possible.

Gandhi had already left for Sevagram, to be surrounded by his "menagerie." There was a special reason for his otherwise baffling haste. Six days before he met Cripps in New Delhi, a unique disciple of his had died—a millionaire devotee whose selflessness, more than anything else, had precluded Gandhi's conversion to Marxism which holds the bourgeoisie as beyond repair and which refuses to reckon with the man under that class label.

The story of Jamnalal Bajaj, long-time treasurer of the Congress Party, is apt to appeal more to the Indian mind than to the Western mind. He was born in an obscure family in a waterless village in the arid State of Jaipur. One of the merchant princes of the State, a man without any offspring, during his aimless wanderings saw the boy, and there and then decided to adopt him as his son and heir. But the poor and principled parents would not part with him until the rich man from Wardha financed the digging of a well for the welfare of the small community.

When Bajaj was seventeen, he did something which aroused his irascible foster-father. Victim of a tantrum, the capitalist reminded the erstwhile poor boy that the latter had come to wealth without working for it. The boy, who later won the Mahatma's affection, showed his mettle in the following letter: "You were so angry with me today. It was God's will, and you had a right to be angry in that you have adopted me. It is not your fault, rather it is the fault of those who gave me in adoption. The money is yours, and you may do whatever you like with it. I am sorry for the expenses you have incurred on me so far, but from this moment I will not touch a pie of your money. . . . I care not for wealth. I pray that I may never forget the name of God who alone can keep me happy in this life and in the next life. And pray be of good cheer and don't sorrow over my going. All earthly relationships are hollow. The worldly possessions hold you in grip. Thank God you have freed me today from their deadly grip. And please rest assured that I will not go to law to claim a pie of what is yours. This is a regular release-deed on a stamped paper, and it declares that you owe me no obligation whatsoever. I owe no debts that you need repay. Use your money in charity, swear not at Sadhus [mendicants] and others, as is your wont, but please them with whatever money you can give. I am taking nothing from the house—nothing but the clothes that cover me." However, he stayed at the insistence of his new father, only to give away in charity five times what he had inherited. Now that he was no more, Gandhi remarked, "Childless people adopt sons. But

Jamnalalji adopted me as father. He should have been an heir to my all. Instead he has left me an heir to his all." Jankidevi, the loving widow, now wanted to burn herself on the funeral pyre as a Suttee, a practice abolished for generations and followed only by a few unusual women even while in vogue. But Gandhi persuaded her to renounce everything and to take up her husband's work. For a life of service must go on.

On May 26, the government raided the Allahabad office of the All-India Congress Committee and seized certain documents to prove that Gandhi was a defeatist. This action was considered extravagant in India. One of the prime principles of the Gandhi movement was that everything should be aboveboard and there must be no secrets. A telephone call from the police department could have summoned the secretaries, loaded with all the files required.

On August 5, Gandhi wrote a personal letter to Chiang Kai-shek in the course of which he stated, "I look forward to the day when a free India and free China will co-operate."

Three days later came the fateful decision of "Quit India," and early next morning Gandhi and others were taken into custody. In the heat and fury of a war which had taken a heavy toll of English soldiers and civilians, in the emotional tides sent bounding against the minds of men by a mortal storm, charges were made that Gandhi refused to resist the Japanese enemy, in spite of Gandhi's proclamation that "I want India to oppose Japan to a man." Such charges were often believed in England and

America, not because of any malice, but because of an inadequate understanding of the Gandhian way of fighting. As Gandhi had fought the British through his Satyagraha, so did he propose to oppose the Japanese by the same weapon. It did not involve the taking of arms, but neither did it involve submission to Japan. Gandhi "would rather be shot."

Another charge was made, that Gandhi was pro-Japanese. But the Mahatma had advised, "Of course, the people must not, on any account, lean on the Japanese to get rid of the British power. That were a remedy worse than the disease." His old friend as well as adversary, Marshal Smuts, came staunchly to his defense, which showed that not all the English-speaking world believed what was being said of the Mahatma amidst the heartbreaks of the war. Said the Marshal: "It is sheer nonsense to talk of Gandhi as a fifth columnist. He is one of the greatest men of the world and he is the last person to be placed in that category. He is dominated by high spiritual ideals. Whether those ideals are always practicable in our difficult world is another question."

That other "question," that sincere doubt as to the practicableness of Gandhi's high spiritual ideals in this difficult world of ours, was haunting even those Western minds which were not staggered by the terrific impact of the war, and who wished India and her saint well. The global imperative was to stem the tide of Fascism so that men like Gandhi would be allowed to live (though occasionally in jail) and to lead men toward larger freedoms. Charitable as they wished to be toward

[185]

a man they knew to be incorruptible, they doubted his sagacity. Wasn't the Mahatma bringing on a civil war just at the moment when all ranks should be closed to face the common enemy whose victory would spell common doom?

That was the supreme charge, and a justified charge. The answer was not a defense but a challenge. It was so unique that it missed fire then, and is likely to miss fire for some time to come; for aftermaths of wars are as evil periods as wars themselves. But it stands there in its stark and unvarnished simplicity for all those who are ready to do some heart-searching.

The Allied concept of war against Fascism was geographic, while the Indian concept of war against Fascism was ideological. The Allied strategy against Fascists was horizontal, based upon national boundaries. The Gandhian strategy against Fascists was vertical; the latter idea was to fight against Fascism wherever it was found in the minds of men. True it is that man has mostly fought geographically. But it is equally true that his gains have been short-lived. Perhaps now is the time for him to learn better and to fight ideologically. Geography has lost most of its meaning in the atomic age.

The Indian struggle became the battle for American public opinion, while Gandhi cooled his heels in a prison. On April 25, 1943, William Phillips, President Roosevelt's special representative to India, announced in a farewell chat, "I should like to have met and talked with Mr. Gandhi. I requested the appropriate authorities for permission to do so and I was informed that they were unable to grant the necessary facilities." His report to his chief, as it was later disclosed, blamed the British more than it did the Indians.

On February 22, 1944, Kasturbai, Gandhi's wife and life-long comrade, died in jail at his side. A handful of close relatives and friends who were allowed to witness the cremation in the compound of the palace turned into a jail, reported that they saw a thing they had never seen before—a tear slipping down the Mahatma's cheek. Wrote Gandhi, "Though for her sake I have welcomed her death as bringing freedom from living agony, I feel the loss more than I had thought I should. We were a couple outside the ordinary. Ours was a life of contentment, happiness and progress."

To paraphrase the familiar dictum that it takes a great man to understand a great man, it took a preposterous Shaw to understand a preposterous Gandhi. Shaw lashed out against the imprisonment of the Mahatma as "the stupidest blunder the Government has let itself be landed in by its right wing of incurable diehards. . . . It [Gandhi's imprisonment] and the unpardonable flogging business associated with it has wiped out our moral case against Hitler. The King should release Gandhi unconditionally as an act of grace unconnected with policy, and apologize for the mental defectiveness of his cabinet."

Gandhi was released on May 6, 1944, but not in the Shavian spirit; he was released "solely on medical grounds." It was all the same to the Mahatma, who felt that the period of reconstruction and co-operation was at hand, and who set about it the day he was free.

XXIII. Hindu, Moslem, and Englishman

Benares is to the East, Mecca to the West; but explore your own heart, for there are both Rama and Allah.

—Kabir

We must all hang together or assuredly we shall all hang separately.

—Benjamin Franklin

Soon after the Mahatma's release, in the closing months of 1944, Mohammed Ali Jinnah, permanent president of the Moslem League, the chief rival of the Congress Party, agreed to come face to face with Gandhi after years of estrangement. Their object was to seek a solution of the Hindu-Moslem controversy which was yearly becoming more bitter.

Only a conference with Winston Churchill, which Gandhi unsuccessfully sought in 1931 while in London, could have been more crowded with incredulity. For, excepting Churchill, Jinnah is the only man who refuses to be impressed by Gandhi's sincerity and saintliness. Other adversaries have succumbed to Gandhi's charm.

Enemies have emerged as friends after a conversation with Gandhi. But not these two men. And no other two men have impeded Gandhi more.

There is only one thing in common between the Mahatma, the Great Soul, and the Qu-I-D-I Âzam, the Great Leader—excessive thinness. But Jinnah is tall. His eyes sparkle with shrewdness. He is very particular about his clothes, wears them well, and is used to having a wardrobe full of famous Bond Street labels. No loincloth for him. He is assertive and strongly opinionated, and his language is challenging and yet engaging. No Mahatma-like meekness about him.

Jinnah was born in 1876, seven years after Gandhi. In India age is respected, but Gandhi must go to see Jinnah. He is a Khoja, and Khojas are recent converts to Islam, very near Hindus. And yet he has become the greatest of Hindu haters. As a lawyer, he gesticulated dramatically, like the late Lord Birkenhead. As a leader, he does the same.

There was a time when Jinnah belonged to the Congress Party and was hailed as an apostle of Hindu-Moslem unity. He was also a social reformer and had little to do with religion. He dressed like an Englishman and married a Parsi woman instead of a Mohammedan. His daughter also married a Parsi. But now Jinnah has disinherited her for doing what he did earlier.

A master of parliamentary debate, Jinnah felt uncomfortable in Gandhi's movement based on direct action. He left the Congress, and went to England. After the death of other Moslem leaders, Jinnah returned and started his move for Pakistan—division of India between a Hindu-India and a Moslem-India.

Most economists and political scientists, Indian and British, agree that Pakistan is impossible. They also feel that it is undesirable in this one world which is seeking larger and larger alignments. If Pakistan is to be the beginning of a Mohammedan Empire embracing the Far East and the Middle East, then too it is bound to fail. For Chinese Moslems are more concerned with being Chinese than Moslem. General Omar Pai Chung-hsi, China's leading Mohammedan general and the spokesman of Chinese Moslems, sent a written appeal to Jinnah urging him to co-operate with the Congress. At the San Francisco Conference, I had talks with delegates from Egypt, Iran, Iraq, Saudi Arabia, Turkey and Syria, and all of them wished Jinnah were more of a nationalist than a separatist. Pan-Arabism has a greater force in the Near East than Pan-Islam.

A compromise between the Moslem League and the Congress is clearly called for. And its realization will undoubtedly be easier once the third party—the British—is eliminated. It is a simple mathematical proposition. To-day the communal problem of India is a static triangle, with the Hindus and the Moslems and the British sitting tight at each angle. When the British quit, the problem will become a mere two-way tug-of-war. I am for a compromise solution, but I am equally eager to see a real and lasting unity based upon an analysis of the root causes of India's divisions.

Hindu, Moslem, and Englishman

Most students of Indian affairs agree that at no time during the British rule was the country seething with as many and as deep inter-group tensions as it is today. In a profound sense, the social problem of cohesion has acquired significance equaled only by the political problem of independence. Unity has become the watchword of Indian leaders, and the lack of unity has become the most oft-repeated phrase in the mouths of British bureaucrats.

The patent explanation advanced by the nationalists is that at long last the British have become conscious of the fact that their domination of India is on its deathbed and that they can prolong the game a bit longer only if they are prepared to play all the trumps that they hold. They are playing it in one vast, final gamble—assert the nationalists. The British are fomenting religious, regional, and class differences as never before. India is seething with countless unacknowledged civil wars as a result.

The patent explanation put forward by the British apologists is that at long last the Indians have become conscious of the fact that they are on the threshold of nationhood and freedom; that, therefore, the tenuous unity engendered by the existence of a common enemy —the British—is evaporating in the thin air of a scramble for power and the seeking of sectional interests; that, for lack of any all-pervading psychological identity, the administrative solidarity fostered by the British is proving too weak to withstand the impact of self-government.

Be it as it may, both these analyses are surface explanations. They do not go deep enough to ferret out stresses that periodically flare up in heightened and marked conflicts. One must go to the roots.

The lead is furnished by the concept of "exclusiveness." Granting that, fundamentally, social differences are the creatures of the contacts between the "in-group" and all other "out-groups," it cannot yet be said that differences themselves are productive of social tensions or social conflicts. True it is that the first contact with unfamiliar ways may produce a shock. Contacts with a different group may cause uneasiness even when the initial shock is absorbed. At the same time, such contacts may lead to amusement with the unfamiliar, intrigued interest with the exotic, and plain admiration for the novel and the new. Moreover, there is a chance of getting accustomed to new ways and even of falling in love with them.

Thus, mere cultural differences are seldom the cause of social conflicts. It is only when these differences are viewed through the glasses of exclusiveness that they become unacceptable, unassimilable, and intolerable. Here a new element is injected, the element of moral judgement. So, at the root of most social conflicts, there lies exclusiveness, a personal and social code that makes fusion impossible by raising an insurmountable moral barrier.

The Hindu is the most tolerant and catholic of religionists. His religion does not predicate a special Hindu god, or a special Hindu heaven. God is one, for Hindus as well as non-Hindus. And any good man can enter heaven; you do not have to be a Hindu to be a good man, nor is every Hindu a good man. There is no dogma of The Way in Hinduism. Various are the ways of approaching truth and realizing God. The result is that Hinduism is the most philosophic of religions, and Hindus have never taken an exception to, let alone persecuted, any alien religion.

Social behavior is a different matter. The Hindu loses his mental flexibility when it comes to life in the community. The doctrine of caste is highlighted by the positive notion of exclusiveness. According to the orthodox doctrine of caste, no intermarriage or inter-dining can take place between two castes, let alone with groups beyond the pale of the Hindu community.

It is true that the caste exclusiveness is losing the social sanctions behind it under the impact of modern life. Even during its heyday, the social patterns created by it were so stylized, ritualized, and accepted by Hindus as well as non-Hindus, that they did not imply any arrogance on the part of excluders and any inferiority on the part of the excluded. But the postulate of superiority was there, to be exploited by those interested in the disunity of India. And it is being brought to the surface of consciousness. The result: a tremendous resentment on the part of the Mohammedans toward the idea of exclusiveness and superiority implied in the Hindu caste system.

The Moslem's case is diametrically different. Socially he is very democratic and it is hard to find any trace of exclusiveness in his behavior. But religiously he is highly exclusive, holding little hope for the salvation of the non-Moslem unless he is converted to Islam. His is an evangelical faith.

One of the tenets of Islam is that in a country not under a Moslem rule, Mohammedan law must prevail over the law of the land in case of a conflict between the two. This implies extra-territorial loyalty and is a political danger-signal with which contemporary Europe and the Middle East are only too familiar. And according to Moslem canon law, the world is divided between *Dur-ul-Islam* (abode of Islam), and *Dar-ul-Harb* (abode of war). The theoretical implications are: that a Moslem cannot live under any regime save a Mohammedan one (although he has done that only too often, historically speaking); that there cannot be peace until the whole world is converted to Islam; that there should be a constant war between the "believers" and the *kafirs*.

It is out of such exclusivistic doctrines, fundamentally, that the Moslem League's proposal of Pakistan springs. But it will be shortsighted to assume that such tendencies of Islam affect India alone, and that they have no bearing on the world at large. For, in the theory of Pakistan, based upon the tenet that the non-Islamic world is the abode of war, are to be found all the rudiments of a new *Lebensraum*, which, in the Nazi ideology, had come to mean not "a place in the sun," but all the space in the sun.

The Englishman in India differs from both the Hindu and the Moslem. If he be a missionary, he is likely to give India a taste not of Christianity, but of evangelical Christianity. And evangelical Christianity is inevitably based upon The Way, The Prophet, The Gospel. All those who do not follow The Way and put the burden of their sins on The Prophet, are lost indeed, and there is no redemption for them. This does not leave any room for live and let live. This makes it impossible for any non-Christian to be a *real* equal of the Christian in India —at least in the eyes of the missionary. Needless to say, there cannot be a greater source of group tension and conflict.

If the Englishman in India is a member of "the ruling race"—a bureaucrat or a civil servant, that is—more likely than not he would draw a circle around his kind and exclude others as "natives."

Now, the term "native" has ceased to be an English word and has become an attitude. It does not so much denote the object as it connotes the holier-than-thou self-description of the subject. It is almost an epithet. When most generously used, the term "native" has an inference of inferiority; when most poignantly used, it has the inference of disdain. It is the precise sense in which Kipling used the word, to show his attitude of superiority, or of disdain, as his spirit moved him, toward the "lesser breeds." So, although he was a great story-teller, Kipling was a poor novelist of India. And the tradition of we-versus-the-natives that he built up has deprived the English language of any great novel of India. E. M. Forster and Louis Bromfield came close to doing it in so far as they repudiated Kipling.

No love or friendship can exist without a feeling of equality—potential if not actual. "Native" lands provide a mere background, a mere locale—as in Kipling, as in Maugham. If there are "native" characters, they are drawn as stereotypes, and not as individuals—the Hindu wife, the Mohammedan bandit, the Tibetan lama, the Indian thug, the Untouchable, the Maharajah, but not Shanta, Ahmed, Surdas, Kadu and Bhimo.

Far be it from me to suggest that Kipling and his sort would never *like* the natives, or at least some of the natives. But since to such mentalities natives are persons to play with, sometimes fondly and sometimes harshly, there are bound to be such aberrations as Kipling's "Gunga Din." The reason Kipling regarded Gunga Din as "a better man than I am" was that the fellow had turned traitor to his own people and sided with their enemies.

Thus the concept of the "native" not only creates linguistic statics; it produces moral storms. Its separatist leanings tend to raise a dual standard of ethical judgement. We may condone something in us that we cannot condone among the natives. Likewise, we may praise a native for doing precisely a thing which, if done by any of *our men*, would dub him a Benedict Arnold.

Differences in mores and folkways may prove shocking but not dividing. The thing that divides mankind in irreconcilable groups is the attitude of "exclusiveness." And exclusiveness is totalitarian and monopolistic. It does not make for peace and understanding. We should be tolerant of everything except intolerance.

PART FOUR: The Future, 1945-

CHARLES: She was like nobody else; and she must take care of herself wherever she is; for *I* cannot take care of her; and neither can you, whatever you may think: you are not big enough. But I will tell you this about her. If you could bring her back to life, they would burn her again within six months, for all their present adoration of her. And you would hold the cross, too, just the same.

CAUCHON: Must then a Christ perish in torment in every age to save those that have no imagination? . . . The heretic is always better dead. And mortal eyes cannot distinguish the saint from the heretic. Spare them.

—*George Bernard Shaw*

And those, Ananda, who either now or after I am dead shall be a lamp unto themselves, shall betake themselves to no external refuge, but holding fast to the Truth as their lamp, and holding fast to the Truth as their refuge, shall not look for refuge to anyone beside themselves—it is they who shall reach the very topmost Height. But they must be anxious to learn.

—*The Buddha according to Hinayana*

XXIV. *Teaching under the Trees*

No man can feel himself alone
The while he bravely stands
Between the best friends ever known
His two good, honest hands.
— Nixton Waterman

We are students of words; we are shut up in
schools and colleges and recitation-rooms for ten
or fifteen years, and come out at last with a bag
of wind, a memory of words, and do not know a
thing.
— Emerson

"I only took the regular course," said the Mock
Turtle.
"What was that?" inquired Alice.
"Reeling and Writhing, of course, to begin
with," the Mock Turtle replied; "and then the
different branches of Arithmetic—Ambition, Dis-
traction, Uglification, and Derision."
— Lewis Carroll

GANDHI set forth what to him looked like "novel" ideas which would "revolutionize education" in India before the All-India National

Education Conference held at Wardha—ideas which will strongly influence the post-war as well as post-Gandhi India.

He advocated learning through doing. The expanding awareness of the child, and its orientation to society, should flow from the hand and the senses to the brain and heart, and from the school to society and God.

Fixing his eyes on a throng that included famous educators and schoolmasters of India, with a number of provincial prime ministers, he said: "The scheme that I wish to place before you today is not the teaching of some handicrafts side by side with so-called liberal education. I want that the whole education be imparted through some handicraft or industry."

Gandhi granted that a similar system existed in the Middle Ages, but that sort of guild training, which served no educational purpose, was not the thing he had in mind. Crafts were then taught for the sake of crafts; they were ends in themselves, and there was no attempt at the development of the mind. "The remedy lies in imparting the whole art and science of a craft through practical training and therethrough imparting the whole education," he added.

Nor did he advocate the methods of modern progressive schools where children are encouraged to play with clay and paint box. "The manual training will not consist in producing articles for a school museum," Gandhi remarked testily, "or toys which have no value. It should produce marketable articles. The children will not do this as children used to do under the whip in the early

days of the factories. They will do it because it enter-
tains them and stimulates their intellect."

Here was a statement of the experience of most creative minds. So many men have found that in using their
hands in some useful but individual work their minds
have functioned best, with thought pursuing thought in
an amazing chain. Not factory work, however, but one-
man vocation alone makes easy such a release of the
mind. This type of work is more apt to stir man to contemplation than the smoke-rings of an armchair philosopher, or the Buddha-like trance of an Indian yogi. And
contemplation, more than any particular study, develops
a world-outlook.

Indeed, as Gandhi says, physical drill, handicraft,
drawing, and music "should go hand in hand in order to
draw the best out of the boys and girls and create in
them a real interest in their tuition." The whole education, he feels, should center around a particular handicraft. Thus history should be taught though the history
of the craft pursued. This should be the starting point
and frame of reference. Instead of memorizing unre-
lated dates and probing the secrets of remote historic
patterns, the child gains historical knowledge through a
central and creative interest. Likewise the learning of
geography, mathematics, physics, social sciences, and
other branches of knowledge are derived from a pursuit
of a chosen craft. Knowledge, instead of stemming from
book or lecture, becomes a creative experience made
possible through creative work. It aims not so much at
literacy as at the literacy of the whole personality.

The yellow cells in the human brain have developed, so psychiatrists assure us, as the result of the use of fingers and thumb. Thought is not independent of action or work. It is only through work that "the whole man" of the Gandhian ideal can emerge. The pursuit of "the whole man," however, is not so novel as Gandhi thinks. What makes his proposal startlingly revolutionary is that the whole man is to be developed through a handicraft. Hand for him holds the secret of mind, and here he is on ground known to modern psychiatrists. The employment of hand in a useful craft not only betrays Gandhi's social consciousness but also his belief that only a socially useful man can be wholly normal.

I do not know how Gandhi would have been received had "thus spake Mahatma" before a Western educational group outside of Columbia's Teachers' College, which is dominated by the thinking of John Dewey and William Kilpatrick. But the conference that Gandhi addressed appointed a committee of recognized leaders of education in India who, after months of toil, produced a plan of basic education embodying his principles. The interest stirred up was so widespread that a year later the government of India appointed its own committee to study the educational system in India. After five years of study and survey, the government committee produced a daring program which bears the unmistakable marks of Gandhi's ideas. But so favorable a response to so unusual a proposal and program cannot be understood save in the light of the checkered history of Indian education.

Teaching under the Trees

In a song of praise addressed to Mother India, Tagore proclaimed:

Thine the skies where dawned the first bright morn,
The hermitage thine where the earliest Samas were sung,
Thine, too, the forest where first went forth sublime,
Knowledge, Religion—Store of Lore Divine.

The Vedas are among the earliest documents of the human mind. Equally true is the fact that the hermitage schools of ancient Aryawarta, Land of the Aryans, where Vedic Samas were compiled and expounded and taught, were among the earliest educational institutions of mankind. These schools were called Gurukulas, or clans of the gurus—a guru being a master-teacher. The master-teachers of ancient India were all forest-dwellers, because a forest, unlike the ocean and the rock, is a growing and speaking thing. Their usual abodes were some shady spot on the Ganges, or on the bank of a lake in the Himalayas, or at the confluence of two or more rivers, since confluence of rivers has ever been for the Hindus a sacred symbol of unity created out of diversity. Under the shadow of the banyan tree, encircled by murmuring bamboo jungles, the gurus lit their sacrificial fires. Around them were their wives, their children, and their pupils. The latter were the flower of Indian youth —heirs to thrones, sons of Bania bankers, Brahmin boys, and future generals, but seldom Shudras, since the schools functioned amidst an aristocratic community. Under the watchful eyes of the gurus, these students grew in sympathy with all creation. They became familiar with the soil under their plows, with the cows that they shepherded in surrounding pastures, with the rabbits and deer that came to their huts for feeding. The birds nesting in thatched huts were their singing companions. The rivers that were stirred by their eel-like splashings as they took their morning baths were intimate living things to them. Communion with nature was the first step toward communion with life's fundamental problems, and direct contact with the guru's own life was the main part of their education in the forest school.

There were several such hermitage schools strewn all over India during the Vedic period. On the Chitrakula hill on river Tamasa was the famous ashrama of Valmiki, the philosopher who is credited with the creation of the epic *Ramayana*. Anangadeva had his Gurukula at the confluence of the Ganges and Saryu. At the confluence of Ganges and Yamuna was situated the Bharadwaja-Ashrama. The Dandakaranya forest, depicted in Thomas Mann's *Transposed Heads*, was studded with many hermitages.

The forest-dwelling master-teachers of Vedic India were rugged individualists, and only occasionally did they get together in a Parishad, whose modern version would be something like a schoolmen's week. Otherwise a hermitage school meant a school of thought, and the master-teacher mostly ran a one-man show. The main note of the hermitage school was intensely personal, and the pupil had the privilege of becoming a real member of the teacher's family. It was the privilege of living in the consciousness of the great mind, and looking at the world through the philosopher's eyes, that distinguished the unincorporated one-man institution of Indian antiquity from organized schools of today. The guru discoursing with his shisyas must have been something like the Plato who did his teaching under a tree at the foot of the Acropolis.

The nature of the institution lent itself to the personal method of imparting knowledge. This put a premium on selectivity both of teacher and pupil. First of all, the teacher had to be not only a master but also a recognized master, otherwise those who could afford it would not go to him in search for knowledge. The requirement of an All-India reputation restricted the hermitage schools to a very small number. There was a further filtering. These schools being one-man affairs were not self-perpetuating; they died with the gurus.

Since there were few teachers and consequently few famous Gurukulas, only the select among the aspirants could attend the institutions of learning. There was, in the first place, the selection based on birth. To that was added, by the gurus themselves, the further selection based on aptitude. It was an extreme form of the tutorial system as practiced in modern times. It trained a class of people to a degree of culture and civilization impossible in a democracy. But it left the masses untouched to a degree also inconceivable in a democracy.

This was the pedagogical pattern of the Vedic India—

of India, that is, of the third millennium before Christ, up to 600 B.C. Then came the Buddhistic revolt. It struck against the privilege of birth but retained the privilege of talent and aptitude. There arose the mighty Buddhist monastic order both for men and women, and this, in turn, introduced for the first time the theory and practice of a corporational educational system. Gradually there grew universities—in the modern sense of the term. These new institutions had organized faculties, and there were endowments and other organizational aspects to bestow upon them the strength of continuity and perpetuity.

Twelve square miles of ruins to the northwest of contemporary Rawalpindi are all that is left of Taksasila, the oldest of India's universities, which flourished between 600 B.C. and 70 A.D. It was world-renowned; it was there that Alexander the Great met Hindu philosophers and teachers of "Taksila." It was at Taksasila that Panini perfected the Sanskrit grammar. And it was Taksasila that trained Chanakya, who wrote his treaties on statecraft and politics which anticipated Machiavelli by fourteen hundred years.

The "crest-jewel of Buddhist heritage" was the University of Nalanda. And what a name! Nalanda means insatiable. It was built between 425 A.D. and 625 A.D. Its ruins are to be found eight miles from Rajgir where Lord Buddha had summoned his first religious congress. Nalanda was composed of six colleges, and it was richly endowed by princes. To Nalanda came the cream of the Indian youth, and scholars thirsting for learning from all over the Near East and also from the Far East. According to the famous Chinese traveler, Hiuen-Tsang, Nalanda was a learned community of 10,000 out of which 1,510 were teachers. Again according to Hiuen-Tsang, at Nalanda were given one hundred different discourses daily. And the Korean, Hwui Lun, who came as a student to Nalanda, tells in his story that he met there scholars from "all countries of Asia."

Although Nalanda provided free education, its office of admissions was an ingenious one. Marking the great campus were four elaborate gates, east, west, north, and south. And at each gate, the Dwarapanditas, or the Gate Scholars, maintained their offices. An aspirant, even if a king's son, had first to pass this hurdle of preliminary examination given by the scholarly gatekeepers.

There were also traditional seats of learning, such as Benares, Ujjain, Kanauj, Tanjore and Kalyana. These were cities studded with small private schools and professional masters. Then there were the schools attached to Hindu temples, to Jaina and Buddhist monasteries, and there were Sanskrit colleges. There were sorts of Chautauqua Weeks moving all over the country in the form of Charakas or wandering students who traveled in groups and debated from place to place. And above all were the Pauranikas, the professional story-tellers, who provided information coated with entertainment to the masses every evening on the town common. There were so many organizations and individuals devoted to the task of imparting knowledge that I-Tsing, the Chinese traveler, remarked that most Indian children "learn the

letters of the alphabet, etc., when they are six years old."
Vincent Smith, the Oxford historian, puts the literacy
figure as high as sixty percent of the population of India
even at that early period.

Then followed the period of decline, confusion, and
a gradual withdrawal from the practical world which
began with the series of invasions that commenced
around 1000 A.D. The period seems to be barren until
the reign of the Mogul emperor, Akbar the Great, who
was a contemporary of Queen Victoria. But his descend-
ants reverted to the old bigotry of the faith, and there
was civil strife and confusion once more. We do not
find any outstanding improvement in the educational
pattern of India until we come to the British period.

The hybrid character of what is loosely called the
British educational system in India owes its origin to the
decade preceding the year 1835 in which English became the official language of India. That decade saw the
famous controversy between the Anglicists and the
Orientalists, the Anglicists advocating the introduction
of the British school system in India, while the Orientalists upheld the traditional curriculum based on the teaching methods of ancient Aryawarta. The Anglicists won.

The charges against the educational system introduced by the Anglicists are many, some unreasonable
and some tenable. Among the proven major complaints
is the one about the unreality of the whole thing. The
system was not rooted in the soil, so all the learning
from the West has remained theoretical in most cases,
to say the least. It failed to prepare Indian youth for the

practical uses to which knowledge can be put. It also tended to denationalize its wards by developing a kind of blind admiration for everything British which, in its turn, gave them a feeling of inferiority for things Indian. Indeed, Indian students got acquainted with Magna Carta and Oliver Cromwell and the British parliamentary system, but the way in which information was imparted failed to light a flame in their hearts to work for similar developments in their own country. The government education in India prepared the student for one thing above all others: to be a clerk in a bureaucracy or in a private firm. Clerkdom is the main profession of most "educated Indians," and in that work a degree counts. As a result, there is an unbearable emphasis on examinations and textbooks. The British system of education has done very little, or much less than it should have in order to answer India's foremost need, to bring Western sciences and technology to India. Moreover, the caste-bound Hindus were bolstered in their mistaken beliefs by the snobbery of the British system. It did not teach the dignity of labor (as the American system does), but instead heaped indignities on labor.

The government system has been operating on such limited scale that after two hundred years only fourteen percent of the Indian population can read and write. And according to Will Durant, the American philosopher of Anglo-Saxon heritage, there were more schools in India before the British came than there are now. The average Indian is perhaps the poorest man in the world with the exception of the average Chinese. And yet under British rule even primary education is neither compulsory nor free. The ancient Hindus based their educational system on the privileges of birth and aptitude. The Buddhists did away with the privilege of birth but maintained the privilege of aptitude. The British did away with both, and instead created the privilege of the pocketbook. Hence India's appalling illiteracy.

For all these reasons, there dawned in India an era of national education. The new trend began with the growth of the early Home Rule movement. Sir Syed Ahmed Khan established the Moslem University at Aligarh. The Aryasamaj founded by Dayananda Saraswati started the Anglo-Vedic College at Lahore, and it strove to relate modern learning with the ancient Hindu heritage. Shradhananda's Gurukula at Hardwar also emphasized the same theme. Then came the Benares Hindu University founded by Pandit Malaviya. All these were private institutions, and in their various ways they strove to re-nationalize the denationalized youth of India. But although they were open to all, they symbolized denominational nationalism—Hindu nationalism or Moslem nationalism—but not an All-India nationalism.

Then came Rabindranath Tagore's international university at Santiniketan, which was founded on the firm basis of an All-India heritage undertaking a free wedlock with modern science and Western thought. But it was limited in its scope if not in its approach, and the real nation-wide revival came only with the Gandhi movement which founded vidyapiths in such strategic places as Ahmedabad, Bombay, Wardha, and Benares.

The Gandhi trend came into its own in 1937 when most of India was being governed by the nationalist party, which had acquired power under the new constitution. Mention has been made of the All-India National Education Conference convened at Wardha that year. Gandhi presided over this body, and it was at that meeting that the program variously known as "Basic National Education," or "Rural National Education through Village Handicrafts," or the "Wardha Scheme of Education," was adopted. It proclaimed, among other things, that:

1. The government should provide free and compulsory education for seven years on a nation-wide scale.

2. The medium of instruction should henceforth be the mother-tongue and not the alien English language.

3. The foundation-principle of this seven-year course should be the one provided by Mahatma Gandhi, namely, "that the process of education throughout this period should center around some form of manual and productive work, and that all the other abilities to be developed or training to be given should, as far as possible, be integrally related to the central handicraft chosen with due regard to the environment of the child."

4. The question of the remuneration of the teachers is bound gradually to be met by this type of semi-self-supporting educational system.

These seven years of primary education were to be the equivalent of the now-known primary, secondary, and high-school training. The bedrock principle of profit-yielding vocation as a means to knowledge as well as a payment of tuition resembled somewhat the Project method in America and the Complex method in Russia. It was designed to make primary education in India free and yet self-supporting in everything except land, buildings, and equipment, which were to be provided by the state. The state was also to guarantee jobs and to buy products of the schools. (This did not take account of higher education which was to be left both to private enterprises and to the state.) But this philosophy of free and yet self-supporting primary seven-year education met two of India's most urgent needs. It made such a venture financially possible in a country suffering from an unhealthy economic system. It also strove to restore the dignity of labor, the absence of which has been one of the greatest curses on India. The ancient Hindus provided education to those who were well-born as well as apt. The Buddhist period provided education to all those who were apt, irrespective of birth. The British provided education to those who could afford it. Now Gandhi was planning to provide education even to those who could not afford it. It is a trend in the direction of democracy. It rejects the qualifications of class, skill, and cash. It guarantees certain basic training to every citizen and forces it even on the unwilling.

The homespun quality of Gandhi's educational plans seems less rustic when his preoccupation with the village is taken into account. India is villages and Gandhi wants her to remain so. He has a peasant's diffidence towards urbanity, and he is unconcerned with the superstructure of any educational system. All he wants is to meet the basic needs of the rural community.

The Wardha Scheme of Education concentrates on a hamlet child of seven and provides a program which would train him until he becomes fourteen. Although it will influence the future of millions of boys and girls, the program is thus limited in its scope. The result is that it is limited also in outlook. It fails to set forth an educational program applicable to higher education and adequate for urban needs.

Gandhi's emphasis on frugality and economy in the schools he proposed had an ironic twist to it. The limited funds that the British made available for education from the Indian exchequer were tied up with the income derived from the government monopoly over drinks and drugs. On the one hand, Gandhi was committed to combatting the evils of intoxicants, while on the other he was anxious to raise the percentage of literacy in India. He had, therefore, to devise a plan which would make education independent of the revenues accruing from sinful sources. The obvious answer, in absence of other income, was self-supporting education.

But there was also a tendency to regard poverty as a badge of honor. The Bania in him has always tended to make a virtue of economy and frugality. When he suggested that the education of the child should center around a craft, he was not merely providing a stop-gap solution to India's poverty. He was advocating, in the words of one of his close disciples, that the child should act as "a citizen from the earliest age at which it begins to show some power of discrimination." Thus a boy is to become a citizen before he becomes a voter. "It is by making the children return to the State," explained Gandhi, "a part of what they receive from it, that I propose to make education self-supporting."

Charges were made that his system would exploit children instead of educating them. Compared to an American boy, an average Indian high-school boy is grave, prematurely grown-up, and preoccupied with politics. By and large, he does not display that playfulness that is the hallmark of growing pains. Nor does he plunge into sports with the abandon of an American. Born old, he would become unhealthily older if harnessed into the Wardha Scheme of Education. The concept of teen-age citizens, adolescents who would "return to the state a part of what they receive from it," is not only un-American, it is un-Brahmin. The Vedic ideal of Brahmacharyashram (celibate studenthood) had conceived the youth to be carefree and the rightful recipient of community attention. From its youth a community draws an insurance policy for its future. The youth should be free of unnecessary obligations, for his whole later life is going to be full of obligations.

Gandhi's insistence on craft training should not sound medieval to an America full of vocational high schools, land-grant colleges, state universities, junior colleges, engineering colleges, normal colleges, and specialized graduate schools far more varied than schools of law, medicine, and theology. But if the aim of education in a free society is to teach students "to think effectively, to communicate thought, to make relevant judgements, to discriminate among values," then the Wardha Scheme of Education, no less than the American over-emphasis on vocational training, will bear fresh appraisal. The question is whether narrow training should be given to youngsters under fourteen years, when they might be, during that formative period, exposed to a flexible and attractive general program? Do not we need well-rounded personalities?

Contradicting his basic philosophy of life, Gandhi sets down a theory of basic education which tends to get away from the humane to the materialistic, from the permanently rational to the temporarily expedient. The answer may not lie in the proposals that take us back to "the classics" and "the humanities." But the answer certainly does not lie in intensification of vocational training.

Gandhi himself was first among those who cried out against the evils of extreme specialization which produced unbalanced personalities. Luckily, it is becoming clearer to some Western thinkers that leaders who are generalizers and integrators are more needed today than are technicians. The era of engineers has made room for the era of managers. Maybe specialization as such has not lost its value; more and more "specialists in generalization" are needed. We need experts, who can view life and the universe as a whole, to chart a way of life compatible with the atomic age. We need more personalities fitted for such life. Would Gandhi's Wardha Scheme produce such personalities?

To Gandhi, the labor-saving device is a crime. To the Western philosopher, A. N. Whitehead, "Culture should be for action, and its effect should be to divest labour from the associations of aimless toil." The poorest result of the Gandhian way of life would be to keep the individual busy with the humdrum routine of existence. The poorest result of the Western way of life would be to render the individual unemployed. Leisure is quite different from forced leisure.

Interwoven with his dislike of labor-saving devices is Gandhi's tenet of non-violence. He advocates a craftsmen's community not because of any love of the primitive, but because he finds it to be a way of life not based on competition and, therefore, not conducive to strifes and wars. War is involved in the machine because the labor-saving effects of the machine engender competition. In his *Armament and History*, Major General J. F. C. Fuller sustains Gandhi by saying, "War is endemic in Western civilization" because of the vicious circle of war and industry. He adds: "Machine power induces unemployment; unemployment increases fighting power; fighting power needs an enemy to justify itself; politics create him, and war systematically follows and for the time being solves the unemployment problem."

Ascetic, frugal and self-denying ways would make competition impossible and exorcise wars. The inevitable fate of an industrial society is war. War is inherent in the manner of our living and of making a living. This notion comes smack against the injunction in Isaiah that we shall not only have life but life abundant. Should man live to the limit of his inventiveness and thus risk periodic wars? Can science save us from science? Or should man exert self-control, practice self-denials, live in a social order frozen at the stage of artisan civilization, and not in a dynamic one which might lead us all to utter annihilation? Can nothing save us from science?

Sometimes I wonder whether wise men of the East do not raise a false conflict between spiritualism and materialism! Sometimes I wonder whether the "realists" of the West are also not posing a false struggle between utilitarianism and idealism! There must be a common ground. Why cannot we combine personal well-being with social service? Why should not a simple way of life be full of comforts? Why must we make a virtue of frugality when there is atomic energy to use—even to waste? Between prohibition and licentiousness is moderation, and between the celibate and the sensualist stands the normal man who has appetites both physical and spiritual. The disciplined man stands in between the seeker and the self-seeker, and discipline is the art of balance.

The literacy campaign outlined in the Scheme of the Central Advisory Board of Education of the Government of India is daring where the Wardha Plan is timid. The educators invited by the government labored for five years, from 1938 to 1944, and they had the co-operation of the delegates sent by Gandhi. Consequently, their proposals retain certain aspects of the training as advocated by the Mahatma. But the government plan has freed itself of the strait-jacket of the Wardha Scheme—its self-supporting plank. The problem is so tremendous that any plan of rapidly educating India's masses will have to be tackled on a mammoth scale.

A breakdown of the 1941 census returns showed that out of India's 389,000,000 only 47,398,000 could read a page. That meant that only 14.5 percent of the population over five years old was literate. A further breakdown revealed that while 22.5 percent of the male population over five years old could read and write, only 5.8 percent of the female population was literate. The disparity between the urban population and villagers who live in some 650,000 rural communities was still more glaring.

Only fifteen universities with 325 "Arts and Sciences" colleges cover British India, as contrasted to the Native States. The number of High, Middle, Primary and Special Schools was 232,264, while there were 85 professional colleges. In 1941, some 15,769,890 Indians were being trained in these 232,789 educational institutions.

Obviously, India's needs are great. Popularly known as the Sargent Plan, the government scheme is inspired with a bigger-and-better American spirit. It proposes to make primary and secondary education free, and it would compel every Indian child between the ages of six and fourteen to attend school. It aims at making all persons below the age of forty literate in twenty-five years. This would require an increase in annual expendi-

ture from the pre-war level of $52,000,000 to $939,000,-
000. And it will call for two million additional teachers.

The plan stresses the industrial needs of India and is
weighted in favor of technological training. As a part of
the program, hundreds of Indian students would attend
technological and industrial schools of America each
year.

XXV. Machines and the Monsoon

*He said, "What seek ye?" They said, "Our
camels."
He said, "Who ever searched for camels on a
housetop?"
They said, "We follow thy example,
Who seekest union with God, while sitting on
a throne."*
                                    —Jalal-uddin Rumi

For the first time in India's
history, a select group of India's leading scientists, industrialists, financiers and statesmen had come together to
form a National Planning Committee to survey India's
human and material resources and to formulate an economic policy which would turn it from a miserably poor
country into one of the richest. Although the committee
was appointed by the Indian National Congress, a political party, officials of the government did not hesitate to
participate. Those were the days of Provincial Auton-
omy, of the Congress success at the polls, of the Congress
rule in eight out of the eleven provinces. It was 1937.
Pandit Jawaharlal Nehru, who was mainly responsible for leading the Congress Party along the lines of

industrial and economic planning, was the chairman of the committee—a vigorous, well-informed chairman. Gandhi had begrudgingly acquiesced, as he often does when the Pandit is adamant. "Pandit Nehru wants industrialization," said Gandhi, "because he thinks that, if it is socialized, it would be free from the evils of capitalism. My own view is that the evils are inherent in industrialism and no amount of socialization can eradicate them."

Gandhi's opposition to industrialization is by no means an objection to economic planning. The Five-Year Plan of Soviet Russia had set the fashion in the field of planned economy. Then came Roosevelt's New Deal to tide over the great depression. As usual, Britain was slow, but finally it too came out with the Beveridge Plan. In India, Sir M. Visvesvaraya carried on a one-man campaign in behalf of planned economy before the Congress decided to appoint the National Planning Committee.

The winds of fashion blowing from the West, however, were not the deciding factor which pushed India so easily along the path of a planned economy. It is in India's tradition. It has been the pattern of Indian polity from times before Christ. The idea of a planned economy was at the core of the Hindu system of caste. The guild system of the medieval Europe was a delayed reflection of the central idea of the caste.

Hindu society was divided into four basic groupings. The pursuits of the Brahmin, or the priest class, were idealistic, emphasizing the purity of the means. The obligations of the Kshatriya, or the warrior community, were altruistic, emphasizing the nobility of the ends. The propensities of the Vaishyas, or the traders, were in the direction of money-making. The Shudras, or laborers, were the workers.

A man's profession as well as status were decided the very moment he was born. He had only a chance to rise higher by his sheer ability in the occupation he was born in; he did not enjoy any freedom to choose his calling. This eliminated competition as a factor in social alignment, and made co-operation based on obedience to caste tenets the force behind all economic activity. The Brahmin got respect but no property. The Kshatriya had social status and honor as his reward. The Vaishya amassed wealth but no honorific position. The Shudra received his salary and pension and he had not a care. The planned economy inherent in caste system maintained a nice balance of occupations, and an equitable mode of immediate distribution. It did not create abundance, but it did foster widespread contentment.

This simple economic organization could function only against the background of idyllic village life. India has been a land of village communities; even today, when urbanization has assailed it, there are 600,000 villages in contrast to a handful of cities. Something akin to the Greek city-states, these village communities were self-governing little republics ruled by panchayat, or the council of five eldermen. Economically they were self-sufficient, their only export trade consisting of surplus goods and artistic specialities. The Committee of Secrecy of the East India Company noted in 1812: "Under this simple form of Municipal Governments, the inhabitants of the country have lived from times immemorial. . . . The inhabitants give themselves no trouble about the breaking up and division of kingdoms; while the village remains entire they care not to what power it is transferred or to what sovereign it devolves; its internal economy remains unchanged."

India, along with China, is the oldest continuous civilization to this day, thanks to village communities. Dynasties have come and gone, empires have fallen and been resurrected, invasions and wars have left their ravages, yet India has remained India because the village was self-sustained and self-governing. Plentiful labor and scarcity of capital led to the rise of village communism, where each one had a duty before he had any right. Karl Marx observes in *Das Kapital*:

"The small and extremely ancient Indian Communities, which still exist to some extent, are based upon the communal ownership of the land, upon a direct linking up of manual agriculture and handicraft and upon a fixed form of the division of labour which is adopted as a cut-and-dried scheme whenever new communities are founded. They constitute self-sufficient productive entities, the area of land upon which production is carried on ranging from a hundred to several thousand acres. The greater part of the products is produced for the satisfaction of the immediate needs of the community, not as commodities; and production itself is, therefore, independent of the division of labour which the exchange of commodities has brought about in Indian society as well. . . . In the simplest form, the land is commonly tilled and its produce is divided among the members of the Community, while every family carries on spinning, weaving, etc., as an accessory occupation. The simplicity of the productive organism in these self-sufficient communities . . . unlocks for us the mystery of the unchangeableness of Asiatic society, which contrasts so strongly with the perpetual dissolutions and reconstructions of Asiatic States, and with the unceasing changes of dynasties. The structure of the economic elements of the society remains unaffected by the storms in the political weather."

The village panchayat maintained its own schools and supervised such public utilities as tanks, wells, roads, rest houses, travelers' inns, town halls. People were close to the soil under a sky unspoiled by smoke. They grew with the trees. To this day India enjoys the legacy of the days of village communism—exquisite buildings, canals, the tanks and lakes, the trunk roads. . . .

The Indian village was the last and the most elusive barrier to the British, who had unseated the Mogul Emperor at Delhi and subjugated his satraps. Land revenue was the principle source of income for the new rulers, and in order to enhance it to its utmost, every individual cultivator had to be reached instead of the village as a whole. Unless the village panchayats were set aside, it was impossible for them to centralize all judicial and administrative powers in their own hands. India, moreover, was looked upon as a producer of raw materials and as a consumer of the finished products made in England. Railways were so organized as to flood the remotest markets with foreign goods. The village panchayats fell, and with them the economic order. It was after this that caste system degenerated into a grading of high and low by the accident of birth.

Gandhi's dream of an artisans' empire, therefore, has an element of revivalism. It is inspired not only by the pastoral charm and beauty of the village that made India, but it also represents resistance to Western encroachment, recompense for the present national shame. This feeling is reinforced by the ugliness of factory towns in Europe and America, by the maladjustments and frustrations produced by the machine in humans not yet ready to cope with its noise and speed and physical exactions, and by periodic wars progressively more scientific to the extent that the next one will be a switchboard affair.

There is *The Gandhian Plan* written by S. N. Agarwal. Gandhi provides a foreword to this brochure in the course of which he writes: "Acharya Shriman Narayan Agarwal . . . happens to be in full sympathy with the way of life for which I stand. This brochure is an attempt to interpret it in terms of modern political science. Acharya Agarwal seems to have made an earnest study of modern literature on the subject. . . . There is no pretence at an exhaustive presentation of the implications of the Charkha [spinning wheel] economics. It claims to be a comparative study of the Charkha economics based on non-violence and the industrial economics which to be paying must be based on violence, i.e., exploitation of the non-industrialized countries."

Agarwal strives to explore the basic demands of Gandhi's program. First among these is the principle of simple living and high thinking. Man becomes more integrated, according to Gandhi, by simplifying his wants and not by multiplying them. It is restraint that is the acme of the art of living, and not unchecked reign of the senses. Gandhi observes, "I do not believe that multiplication of wants, and machinery contributed to supply them, is taking the world a single step nearer its goal. . . . I wholeheartedly detest this mad desire to destroy distance and time, to increase animal appetites and to go to the ends of the earth in search of their satisfaction." Comforts make men soft, easy-going, and even selfish. Their values become materialistic and civilization is measured in terms of the number of bathtubs and air-conditioned movie houses.

Complexity of wants produces complexity of tools, and here another of the Gandhian demands enters. Increased wants inspire mass production. Fewer and fewer produce more and more. They come in contact only with a small process, day after day. They themselves become tools. As a result the element of creative delight in one's work is lost. One must seek creative satisfaction somewhere else, and there arises that schizophrenia, the split, of modern life wherein work is regarded as a necessary evil and the pursuit of happiness starts after 5:00 P.M. Pistons are substituted for hands, and assembly lines for feet, but, according to Gandhi, our real happiness and health come from a proper use of our hands and feet.

Gandhi would substitute for mass production the production by masses. To him labor is the law of nature, an obligation for every man. "It is a tragedy of the first magnitude," writes Gandhi, "that millions have ceased to use their hands as hands. Nature is revenging herself upon us with terrible effect for this criminal waste of the gift she has bestowed upon us as human beings." He insists that all men should do physical work, at least for a few hours a day if their occupations are intellectual. I remember that at his university students and professors of politics had to do carpentry for two hours each school day.

This doctrine has a special meaning for India. In India, the principal resource is labor, which is going to waste. India's problem, therefore, is how to convert labor into wealth. The American emphasis on labor-saving devices stems from the days of the early settlers when labor was scarce and nature bountiful. Men should replace machines in India. This is what is meant by the Gandhian notion of production by masses as opposed to mass production.

An example is the world-famous Kashmir shawl that "passes through an engagement ring." It is illustrative of how wealth is created by labor. It is made in families who have pursued the profession for generations. The woolen cloth itself hardly costs twenty dollars. But ten to fifteen people will work on it for three to six months.

The grandfather sits in a corner singing songs which contain the formula for the pattern desired, and a hundred fingers deftly follow the lyrical message, now using red thread, now blue. A rainbow of color and an exquisite pattern of embroidery emerge when the work is completed. The twenty dollars worth of wool is then sold for several hundred.

Sanctity of labor which provides creative delight, therefore, is another of Gandhian economic postulates. Closely tied up with this is his fear of the lure of leisure. Says he, "Leisure is good and necessary up to a point only. God created man to eat his bread in the sweat of his brow, and I dread the prospect of our being able to produce all that we want, including our foodstuffs, out of a conjurer's hat." Not only he is against labor-saving devices; he proposes that each man should be as self-sufficient as possible. The ideal distribution of a day, according to Gandhi, would be eight hours' sleep, eight hours' work, and eight hours' leisure for cultural and social pursuits.

Gandhi places human values above economic values. Like Ruskin he scorns the economic principle which says "Buy in the cheapest market and sell in the dearest." That cheap market might have been created by the blood of the working class, and in trying to sell at the highest price you can get you might become the cause of several deaths. Thus finally enter into Gandhi's economic picture his principles of non-violence and the belief that all centralization is based on force. "I suggest," says Gandhi, "that if India is to evolve along non-violent lines, it will have to decentralize many things. Centralization cannot be sustained and defended without adequate force. Rurally organized India will run less risk of foreign invasion than urbanized India well equipped with military, naval, and air forces."

One feels that in his worship of the village Gandhi is after the purest form of democracy. "The only Government," wrote John Stuart Mill, "which can fully satisfy all the exigencies of the Social State is one in which the whole people participate."

Village economy is of necessity agricultural economy. But Gandhi is more than an Indian Thoreau in search of a Walden, and he realizes that farming in India is tied up with the monsoon. The rainy season lasts only four to five months a year, and it is during those monsoon months that all the farming is done in India. For the greater part of the year, therefore, the Indian farmer is idle. To utilize his idle months and thus to increase his income, Gandhi has evolved a plan of providing him with such small industries and crafts that he can pursue in his cottage on the farm. As there will be goldsmiths and ironsmiths and potters in the village, there will be farmers turned into artisans in farmhouses. Production at this stage is almost simultaneous with consumption and distribution, thus avoiding the iniquities of capitalism. S. N. Agarwal lists among industries subsidiary to agriculture: animal husbandry; dairy farming; tanning and leather work; fruit culture; vegetable gardening; forest industries. Among cottage industries the following are outstanding: spinning and weaving cloth; paper-making; seed-oil extraction. The All-India Spinners Association, and the All-India Village Industries Association, both started by Gandhi, are already popularizing these methods of making the village thoroughly self-sufficient. Such basic industries as power, mining, small machinery, heavy engineering, and chemicals would be owned and operated by the state, and so would all public utilities.

If Ruskin could not halt England's industrialization, can Gandhi stave off India's march toward mass production? Gandhi is a leader of men, the most powerful influence in India, possessing the persuasive power of a hundred Ruskins. Yet his back-to-nature cry is a cry in the wilderness simply because the powers he must contend with have no wish to be converted. Technology is amoral. All it displays is an irrepressible onward urge. Its progress is accumulative, not selective. It has, like all means, only one criterion—higher efficiency. There is no going backward in science or technology. The Potsdam plan to turn industrial Germany into a pastoral one, one of the most audacious objectives in the history of man in society, had to be abandoned before a trial. There was force at the disposal of the Big Three, and Gandhi has no such force to compel India nor would he use it even if he had it. It is not contended that a stop to scientific invention could never be attempted. Nor do I believe that it is impossible always for men in society to go back to a simpler technology. But to do so would require a greater moral force than the blind force of science, and could come only out of the organized effort of a majority of mankind.

The idea of self-sufficiency, be it on the individual or village or national level, implies a regionalism and isolationism made impossible in an age where "the basic power of the universe," as President Truman put it, is invoked and unleashed. Gandhi derives his inspiration, I believe, from Indian culture since Buddha. The science of nuclear physics, which has freed atomic energy, is in harmony with even older India, India of the Vedas whose doctrine of advaita, or monism, regarded purush and prakriti (matter and energy) as one and the same.

The economics of asceticism is the economics of scarcity. It is restricted and austere. Although an energy system, it is a low energy system. It is adaptive, takes for granted things as they are—nature as it is—and tries to make the best of it. In contrast, science represents a high energy system. It is creative rather than adaptive; it does not follow nature. It tries to master nature by discovering natural laws. It would refuse to gear Indian economy to the caprices of the monsoon; it would irrigate the land instead. Once they know it, most men would prefer a high energy system to a low energy system. It is true that modern technology has increased and intensified wars. Gandhi would scuttle modern technology. Those who function on a high energy system, both in the East and particularly in the West, would suggest not a negative means of denial but a positive solution of a cosmic equation for the atomic bomb through the organization of men's minds toward peace.

XXVI. India and the World

A tool is but the extention of a man's hand, and a machine is but a complex tool. He that invents a machine augments the power of man and the well-being of mankind.

—H. W. Beecher

WHITHER India? Is India outgrowing the Mahatma? Or growing away from him? The trend is unmistakable, especially in the field of industrialization. *The Gandhian Plan* may continue to serve as a gadfly and may even exert influence here and there, but it seems that it has already taken a minor place in relation to another plan which has fired the imagination of the people.

Making fruitful use of the material gathered and suggestions made by the National Planning Committee, a group of Indian industrialists and businessmen has produced a proposal entitled *A Plan of Economic Development for India*. It is popularly known as the Bombay Plan.

The unorthodox attitude of Indian industrialists toward the concept of a planned economy is perhaps in sharp contrast to that of financiers in Western democracies. While industrial and financial magnates in other countries, especially in the United States, are grumbling against increasing government control and planned economy, in India the industrial and financial tycoons themselves are proposing a plan which would subject them to such controls.

There is a reason behind the tremendous enthusiasm inspired by the Bombay Plan. People realize that only a planned economy can cure India of the existing lopsided economy. India is one of the most poorly industrialized areas in the world. Only five percent of the population is supported by industry, and a mere four percent employed in factories and plants. An overwhelming proportion of the people, eighty-three percent to be exact, eke out a precarious existence from the soil—a soil overworked and overpopulated, a soil mostly unpaying because of the ridiculous smallness of the average Indian farm, which is three acres. Agricultural economy is true to the pattern of colonial rule.

The result is inevitable. The average per-capita income in India is estimated at $26 per year. But India is a land of staggering contrasts, and five of the fifteen richest men in the world come from India. The Nizam of Hyderabad is reputed to be the richest man on earth, so the average income is also a poor index. The mean income of India is much less than $26. The picture of India is that of periodic hunger, of masses living below subsistence level, of chronic under-employment and unemployment, of lack of sanitation and adequate medical care, of few schools, of dirt and disease.

The plan of cottage industries such as Gandhi proposes is held as an inadequate solution. One sure means of bettering things is to remove a part of the population from agriculture and to absorb it, along with the unemployed, in factories. That means many more factories. Hence the enthusiasm among thinking Indians for industrialization. They, unlike Gandhi, believe that a balance must be struck between agriculture and industry.

The principal aim of the Bombay Plan is "to bring about a doubling of the present per capita income within a period of fifteen years." But since each year India must feed five million more mouths, the doubling of the per-capita income over a period of fifteen years will necessitate a trebling of the present national income. In dollars and cents, the present yearly national income of some $8,250 millions should be increased, in fifteen years, to some $24,750 millions.

With a view to coupling the increase in India's wealth with a progressively more balanced economy, the Bombay Plan proposes only to double the present agricultural output while quintupling the industrial one. In the initial stages priority will be given to such basic industries as electricity, mining and metallurgy, machinery and machine tools, chemicals, armaments, and transport. For only on the foundations of electric power and capital goods can an ever-expanding industrial superstructure be built.

Although Gandhi is fighting a losing battle, he is

bound to leave two salutary effects on the shape of factories to come and on the nature of subsidiary industries to be set up. His protestations are likely to inspire Indian enterprisers (as late-comers in the field of industrialization) to learn not only from American and European successes, but also from their mistakes. There need not be, for instance, large factory towns with their attendant slums, cesspools, dirt, and disease. Henry Ford's vision has met Gandhi's nostalgia for nature at least halfway. India can apportion her industries and distribute her new factories over the countryside, so that even industrial workers would retain the healthy touch of soil. That would be sound, too, from the point of view of national defense.

Gandhi's influence is bound to be more direct as to the second modification. There need not be a total abolition of cottage crafts and industries, such as has taken place in highly industrialized nations of the West. Even when India strikes a balance between agriculture and industry, a predominant part of the population will be doing farming. They can use their spare hours in cottage industries and increase national wealth as well as add to their individual incomes. The Bombay Plan has welcomed their beneficial effects in "reducing the need for capital, particularly of external capital." This constitutes a happy compromise between Nehru's modernism and Gandhi's agrarianism.

Believing that "it does not follow that increased production will necessarily remedy the problem of poverty if it is not based on a proper system of distribution," the

Bombay planners have taken up the question of equitable sharing of benefits. To insure this, they see it will be necessary to have state control, but only to prevent private enterprise from becoming acquisitiveness. Control should have a double purpose: to secure for everybody a minimum income, and to prevent gross contrasts in income. The latter can be accomplished by decentralizing the ownership of the means of production, by imposing death duties, by encouraging the widespread distribution of shares in joint-stock companies, by regional distribution of industries, and through the development of co-operative enterprises. The state, if fully responsible to the people, is expected to control and own basic industries and public utilities, according to this plan, as according to *The Gandhian Plan*.

The ubiquitous demand for India's industrialization, however, should not create an impression that there are no industries in the country. In fact, she has already made a very good start. India has 41,000 miles of railroads. She holds almost world monopoly over the jute industry. Her textile industry is the second largest on the globe; annually 4,500,000,000 yards of cloth are woven in the mills of Ahmedabad and Bombay. She has a growing cement industry, and her sugar industry is the largest in the world. India's steel industry is the second largest in the British Empire, and the Tata Steel Works at Jamshedpur are the largest in the British Empire. Believe it or not, Indians take their turbans off only to Hollywood; India is the second largest producer of movies in the world. Already considered the sixth largest industrial country in the world, India aspires to become the third.

India has two other assets—manpower and mineral resources. Americans in charge of construction in the China-Burma-India theatre of war invariably found that Indians took to machines very easily. And India's natural wealth is also enviable. It is estimated that India is the richest country in the world in deposits of high-grade iron ores. North India possesses a great and unexploited oil area, and the Central Indian coal deposits can compare favorably with those of most countries. Three-fourths of the world's supply of mica, and one-third of the world's supply of manganese come from India. A vast timberland, she annually produces 500,000 tons. India produces enough staples for its teeming humanity in normal times, importing only 140,000 tons of rice from Burma. She is the second largest grower of cotton, and the largest grower of tobacco in the world.

Taking account of these assets of India, the Bombay planners estimate that the fifteen-year haul that they propose in the fields of industry, agriculture, communications, education, health, and housing is going to cost India some $37,000 millions. These are astronomical figures from the point of view of a people still unfamiliar with the "American talk." So the Indian brain-trusters discarded the classical theory of money and postulated that "the real capital of a country consists of its resources in material and manpower, and money is simply a means of mobilizing these resources and canalising them into specific forms of activity." Other financial sources at India's disposal are: hoarded wealth of the country, mainly gold; savings of the people; new money created against *ad hoc* securities.

This will largely take care of internal finance, but India will have to have some external currency for the first stage of her fifteen-year industrialization program. In the initial years, she will have to buy machinery from the United States and pay in cash. In this connection, Indian economists are banking heavily on the possibility of converting their country's sterling balances in London into universal purchasing power.

At the end of the World War II, India's claims against British blocked sterling stood around $5,000,-000,000. This balance to the credit of India in a London ledger represented blood, sweat, and tears on the part of India's masses who were forced to live under sub-human standard (through a lack of civilian goods), so that the grist would be forthcoming for the mills of Allied defense. And this balance also represented goods and services given by India over and above the huge sum she spent on her own defense. It represents not only the price of the Indian goods that Great Britain took away, but also the price of the goods and services that India gave to Australia, Canada, Iran, and China. India did not receive any direct payments from these countries; England collected them and then issued IOU's to India.

Moreover, what the United Kingdom admitted to be her public debt to India was only a part of her actual financial obligation. For Great Britain had already sub-

tracted, or realized, India's alleged pre-war public debt
to England, estimated at $1,800,000,000—a public debt
whose major part should not have existed in the first
place. For even the expenses due to the wars of the
East India Company and latterly of the British Government under the Crown, incurred mainly to conquer
India and to consolidate British control first over India
and then over Burma on the one hand and areas beyond
the Northwest Frontier on the other, were placed on
the stooping shoulders of Mother India as her public
debt to England. Thus India was required to pay for
the very chains around her wrists. The public debt was
further increased by saddling India with the expenses
incurred by England for her own expeditions in Af-
ghanistan, Abyssinia, China, Persia, Egypt, Malaya,
Java, Ceylon, and Cape Colony. From these, India had
nothing to gain except the ill will of those freedom-
loving peoples.

India was even denied full use of her dollar resources,
which had been accruing to her because of her increasing trade in private merchandise with the United States.
All such dollar credits were put in the so-called Empire
Dollar Pool. By the end of World War II, these credits
amounted to over a billion dollars. It was evident that if
these credits had been made available to Indian buyers,
greater trade would have resulted between America and
India. India was, however, a man with a billion-dollar
balance in the bank but not enough cash to pay his taxi
fare.

In view of the fact that Great Britain could pay

neither in cash nor in kind acceptable to India, it is demanded that Britain enable India to convert annually around $70,000,000 of her sterling credit into American dollars for the industrialization of her land with the aid of U. S.-made capital goods, and that $1,250,000,000 worth of British investments in India be transferred to the Government of India.

Leaving behind the pastoral life glorified by Gandhi, and about to enter her iron age, India's eyes are riveted on America with a view to collaboration for mutual profit. A trek to America has started—by scientists, by businessmen, by industrialists, by government officials, by students, by nationalist leaders. The ancient philosopher has come to the door of the young industrial giant.

In the raging controversy over international trade policies, India is closer to America than to England. For instance, India supports the American stand in behalf of a multilateral trading system. For India has suffered economically under the British policy of imperial preference. This is not a closed-door policy, but it can indeed be described as a back-door policy. It is a sort of tariff system based on regionalism rather than on nationalism, and it involves a disguised form of barter. There are higher duties on India's imports from the United States than on India's imports from Great Britain. India feels that empire preference is restrictive not only of her own trade, but also of world trade.

In the field of currency relations and international exchange, Indian economists have developed a sixth sense. Their mastery over this particular set of problems can be ascribed to the anomalous position of the Indian rupee. For the Indian rupee is a monetary minor, tied to the apronstrings of the pound sterling; it cannot directly be computed into American dollars. And by a constant policy of appreciating the exchange value of the rupee, the British government has followed a course of British betterment to the detriment of Indian interests. An appreciated rupee means a better opportunity for the British import trade in India, better terms for remitting salaries and profits earned by British officials and businessmen in India. Looking for an opportunity to cut loose the rupee from the pound sterling in order to terminate an incompatible marriage, India is for an internationally stabilized currency.

India's stand against international cartels is due to the pressing need to protect her nascent industries and to start new ones. There are several stumbling blocks lying on this path, one of which is the cartel system. When India attempts to get new plants going, international cartels try to prevent her from securing protective tariffs. India at present believes that free trade is a luxury only advanced nations can afford. A nation newly on the path of industrialization would need protective tariffs, at least temporarily. In many instances when Indians succeeded in securing increased tariffs, the cartels have stepped in and set up their own plants. These plants would operate at a loss, which would be absorbed by the parent company. India knows too much.

Among the oft-suggested economic contributions to world peace is the new-fangled slogan of "equal access to raw materials." It is presumed that by some inherent magic this doctrine will eliminate international trade rivalries and curb national greeds. What is forgotten is that only highly industrialized nations propound this doctrine since it benefits only them and works to the detriment of those who are technologically backward. It is natural for highly industrialized countries to seek raw materials in terms of regularity and security of supplies at cheap prices. But this would not only maintain but also intensify the division between the manufacturer of finished products and the producer of raw materials. Being a producer and consumer, as well as an exporter of raw materials, India is opposed to the policy of open door to raw materials.

The main grievance of India in the field of transportation concerns maritime activities. In spite of a long and proud tradition of shipping, and a coastline of nearly four thousand miles, Indian-owned tonnage comes to little over 135,000; it represents only 0.24 percent of the total world tonnage. All in all, Indians own sixty-five ships. Hardly five percent of the total coastal and overseas trade is carried by Indian shipping. Indian interests are therefore demanding: India's shipping should be protected by coastal reservations; and international shipping policy should provide room for a national mercantile marine commensurate with India's trade.

Indian industrialists have indicated that their country will deal more and more with the United States. America can supply India with the technical know-how. In return, India can provide a market for the capital goods made in the United States. India can also provide employment for thousands of American engineers and technicians. America's commercial frontier can still be found on the Ganges.

But India is interested in more than a bilateral agreement with the United States. She is interested in a world-wide commercial scheme. That is why she took such a constructive part at Bretton Woods in spite of the fact that she lost out on two important counts there. The first defeat came in connection with the proposed International Monetary Fund. Her quota is the sixth largest, totaling $400,000,000. The first five nations— United States, Great Britain, Russia, China, and France —have acquired what amounts to automatic representation on the governing board. In view of India's tremendous national wealth and great industrial potential, she should have been given more consideration. The second defeat came in connection with the proposed International Bank for Reconstruction. The difference between the French quota and the Indian quota to the monetary fund is only $50,000,000 (and India is willing to increase her quota, but is not allowed), but that slight margin entitles France, as one of the five having the largest number of shares, automatically to elect an Executive Director, while India, being sixth, has no such privilege. This maneuver was more political than economic, and was a clear sign of discrimination.

India put down this first misadventure in internationalism to her status as a subordinate of Britain. Soon followed a similar setback for the same reason, but this time in the political field. At San Francisco, India failed to receive a permanent seat on the Security Council of the United Nations Organization as the Big Sixth, although the logic of power, area and population entitled her to that position.

Yet the trend is toward international co-operation. It is a policy more closely identified with Nehru, but Gandhi is not opposed to it. There is, however, a curious personal dilemma involved so far as the Mahatma is concerned. India is drawn toward a world organization which is pledged to use violence when international peace is threatened. Internally also, political observers have noticed the people of India to be in a new mood. Nehru has advocated a revolution and, although there has been no open call to violence, a new undertone is noticeable in the utterances of other leaders. Will India remain what the Mahatma wants her to be—an example of peace in a warring world? What is in store? What strange denouement . . .

The Parable

In WESTERN INDIA there is a "Sinners' Temple" with an ironic legend. The story should be told here.

When I saw it, in 1933, it appeared to be more a walled-in sanctuary than the customary Hindu temple. In the center of the compound stood the stump of a neem tree, blackened and charcoaled, as if burnt by lightning. On one side of the stump stood a small monument which the devotees called the Shrine of the Sinner, while on the other was a row of seven tombs known as the Shrine of the Seven Saints.

As I stood there I noticed that when the villagers came to worship, they threw stones at the Seven Saints, and then went to the Shrine of the Sinner and placed flowers on the altar.

The priest noticed my bewilderment, as he must have observed the wonder of many other pilgrims before me. . . .

It happened during the monsoon of the year 1921 . . . the terrible monsoon that brought "green famine" by inundating the land. In those days there stood a temple whose ruins could still be seen not far from this curious sanctuary. In that temple reigned a famous priest whose habit it was to gather together the seven elders of the village every evening and to discourse with them on the ways of men, and on right and wrong.

One evening, when they were assembled in the temple, a sudden thunderstorm broke in fury over the village. The torrents beat against the windowpanes. The lightning flashed over the temple continuously, but did not strike. It seemed as though the lightning were hovering over the heads of the eight men in the temple, trying to find a victim.

With profound seriousness, the renowned priest, wise in the ways of mysterious powers, spoke up: "As all devotees of God know, lightning always strikes the sinner. That has been the observation of wise men from olden times even until now. I have a feeling in my heart that there must be a sinner amongst us whom the lightning is seeking. Fearful of killing the remaining seven servants of God, it is hovering over our heads and not striking. So I suggest that each one of us go, one by one, and touch that neem tree in the temple yard. The sinner will be thus sorted out and struck by the lightning, but at least seven others will be saved."

The group agreed that the priest's advice was sound. So one by one they made the fateful trip. Six of them came back unharmed, and still the lightning flashed and hovered overhead.

Except for the priest himself, there remained only the village money-lender, an old and wise man. It was his custom to wander from farmhouse to farmhouse collecting his debts while he sang songs in praise of God. Often he would come back empty-handed lest he deprive poor farmers of their daily bread. So people called him, behind his back, the "Fool of God."

Presently he got up to make the trip to the neem tree. But the priest, blocking the way, said to the money-lender, "All the countryside knows that you are unlike other money-lenders and that you are a real servant of God. So, if there is a sinner between us two, it must be I."

Without waiting for an answer, the priest ran to the tree. And still the lightning did not strike.

By the time the priest came back, all the rest were excited. They had begun to feel that the money-lender was a cheat who, under the cloak of saintliness, must have practiced deceit and exploited the poor and ignorant farmers through trickery. This suspicion was confirmed by the priest himself who remembered suddenly that the "Fool of God" had collected his loan to the temple in full.

Thereupon, silent and crestfallen, the money-lender walked across to the neem tree. As he touched the trunk, there was a blinding flash in the sky, followed by deafening thunder.

The lightning struck.

The lightning did not strike the money-lender touching the tree; it instantly destroyed the seven men in the temple.

LIBRARY
SOUTHERN SEMINARY